HOPETOUN

Scotland's Finest Stately Home

HOPETOUN

Scotland's Finest Stately Home

Edited by

Countess of Hopetoun
Polly Feversham
Leo Schmidt

Foreword by

The Marquess of Linlithgow

Contributions by

Anne Bantelmann-Betz, Peter Burman, Christopher Dingwall, Asita Farnusch,
John Hardy, James Holloway, Lord Alexander Hope, Earl of Hopetoun, David Jones,
Alexandra Skedzuhn-Safir, and Christoph Martin Vogtherr

Photographs by

Frank Dalton and Claire Takacs

HIRMER

The Hope Family

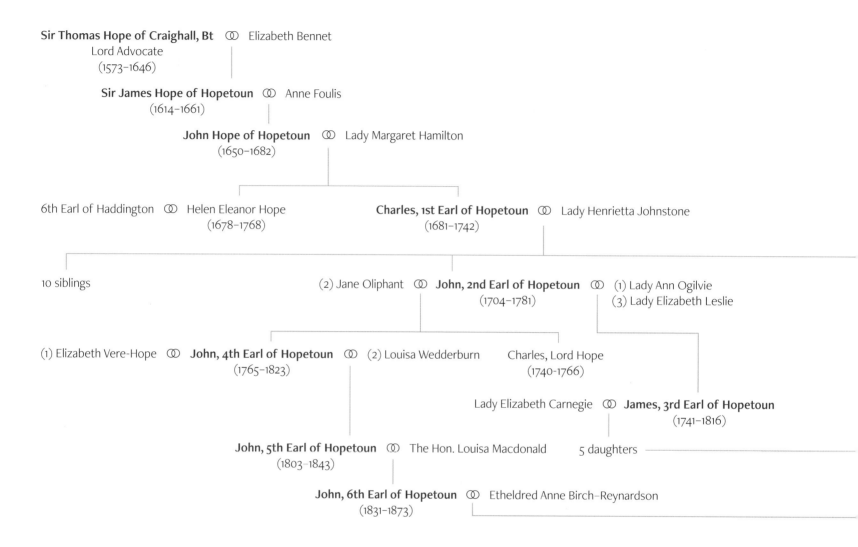

Sir Thomas Hope of Craighall, Bt ⬭ Elizabeth Bennet
Lord Advocate
(1573–1646)

Sir James Hope of Hopetoun ⬭ Anne Foulis
(1614–1661)

John Hope of Hopetoun ⬭ Lady Margaret Hamilton
(1650–1682)

6th Earl of Haddington ⬭ Helen Eleanor Hope
(1678–1768)

Charles, 1st Earl of Hopetoun ⬭ Lady Henrietta Johnstone
(1681–1742)

10 siblings

(2) Jane Oliphant ⬭ **John, 2nd Earl of Hopetoun** ⬭ (1) Lady Ann Ogilvie
(1704–1781) (3) Lady Elizabeth Leslie

(1) Elizabeth Vere-Hope ⬭ **John, 4th Earl of Hopetoun** ⬭ (2) Louisa Wedderburn   Charles, Lord Hope
(1765–1823) (1740–1766)

Lady Elizabeth Carnegie ⬭ **James, 3rd Earl of Hopetoun**
(1741–1816)

John, 5th Earl of Hopetoun ⬭ The Hon. Louisa Macdonald   5 daughters
(1803–1843)

John, 6th Earl of Hopetoun ⬭ Etheldred Anne Birch-Reynardson
(1831–1873)

Charles Hope-Vere ⚭ Catherine Vere
(1710–1791)

The Families of Hope Vere and Hope Johnstone,
Earls of Annandale

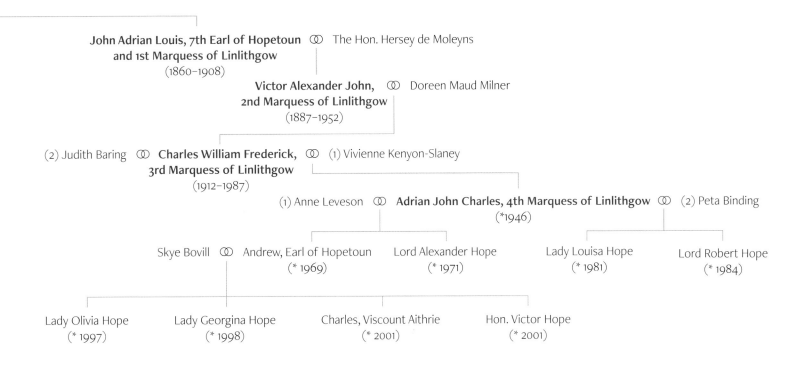

John Adrian Louis, 7th Earl of Hopetoun ⚭ The Hon. Hersey de Moleyns
and 1st Marquess of Linlithgow
(1860–1908)

Victor Alexander John, ⚭ Doreen Maud Milner
2nd Marquess of Linlithgow
(1887–1952)

(2) Judith Baring ⚭ Charles William Frederick, ⚭ (1) Vivienne Kenyon-Slaney
3rd Marquess of Linlithgow
(1912–1987)

(1) Anne Leveson ⚭ Adrian John Charles, 4th Marquess of Linlithgow ⚭ (2) Peta Binding
(*1946)

Skye Bovill ⚭ Andrew, Earl of Hopetoun   Lord Alexander Hope   Lady Louisa Hope   Lord Robert Hope
(* 1969)   (* 1971)   (* 1981)   (* 1984)

Lady Olivia Hope   Lady Georgina Hope   Charles, Viscount Aithrie   Hon. Victor Hope
(* 1997)   (* 1998)   (* 2001)   (* 2001)

Table of Contents

Foreword

by The Marquess of Linlithgow

Hopetoun has been, and remains, my family's home since we built it over 300 years ago. I now live in another house on the estate, but Hopetoun was, for many years, my own home; my son and his family live there now. It remains a source of great pride to me that our forebears created such an outstandingly beautiful piece of architecture. It is the masterpiece of two of Scotland's leading architects, but also of Earls of Hopetoun who were passionate about building and the creation of this wonderful place. The two architectural styles, that of Sir William Bruce and the Adam family, sit well alongside one another in the same way the house sits easily within the grounds and wider landscape. They combine and contrast to give the beautifully tranquil atmosphere that to me has always been such an essential part of its character.

This would be of little more than academic interest if the house were not still a living entity. It has been owned since 1974 by an independent charitable trust, the Hopetoun House Preservation Trust, on the board of which I and my eldest son sit as Trustees. The Trustees conserve and steward the building with the team, to whom we are all indebted, whilst the family owns and manages the surrounding estate; the combination allows Hopetoun to remain true to its original purpose whilst adding an entrepreneurial spirit that supports and underpins it. I believe this combination of the traditional with the forward-looking can secure its future, hopefully for at least another 300 years.

As well as a pride in the place, Hopetoun often raises in me a desire to know more about its building and decoration. Why were the decisions made that led to the end result? How were the conflicting and competing priorities balanced? The house when first seen is so clearly a product of the Georgian era, with its taste for the magnificent, that it comes as a surprise to some how comfortable and relatively practical many of the interior spaces are. I am pleased to find that some of these questions are addressed in the various chapters of this book.

Since its building, Hopetoun has been well studied, and many books have been written about or including it. This book will sit deservedly amongst them and contribute greatly to the canon.

Introduction

by the Countess of Hopetoun

A s with most of the great buildings in the United Kingdom, much has been written over the years about Hopetoun, but this is the first monograph to explore it with such a wide-ranging approach. The research in this volume is of exceptional depth, breadth, and calibre, giving it a place alongside the most eminent of its fellows. The book, the result of years of careful archival research and on-the-ground investigation, unravels some of the complexities of a house built in two parts with two very different approaches by two of Scotland's leading architects, William Bruce and William Adam, but for the same client. The theme of the Patron, as the guiding hand and aesthetic controller, is a recurrent one within the chapters that follow, which discuss the house itself, the surrounding landscape and buildings, the furniture, furnishings, paintings, and contents. The Patron role has passed from generation to generation through the years (including, albeit in a less wide-ranging and more restricted way, the present and hopefully future generations as well), and the resulting layers, so many of which are still visible, are what help to create the unique atmosphere felt throughout Hopetoun.

It is increasingly rare for a home to continue to be lived in by the family that built it, and in a way that would, at least in part and at certain times of the year, be recognisable to the previous generations. One of the joys of Hopetoun, and something that makes it especially interesting to study and research, is that everything within the walls has been designed, conceived, commissioned, collected, or bought by a continuing line of one family. The archives are a treasure trove of receipts, invoices, and letters discussing decisions; the fact that these primary sources are available, and *in situ*, has made research even more exciting, intimate, and human. The story of Hopetoun is as much the story of the Hope family and their changing style, taste, and aspirations as it is of the talented designers who supplied the technical or artistic skills that made it possible. This is referred to by most of the contributors, who acknowledge the importance of an overarching continuity.

Sitting on the edge of the Firth of Forth, Hopetoun has long dominated its surroundings, and continues to do so even with the construction of the toweringly elegant new Forth Crossing designed by Naeem Hussain. The house was always intended to make an impact, but it does so in a way that emanates hospitality. There is a surprising contradiction between the scale of the house and the warm impression as the colonnades encompass you on arrival. It is a friendly house; charmingly, the late Duchess of Devonshire described the wings of Hopetoun as being like arms reaching out to welcome you. Even the carefully designed front steps have an easy feel to them, the depth and height of tread being perfectly considered and executed. The hall is austere, almost spartan, whilst the enfilade of state rooms running north are decidedly grand, contrasting markedly with the interiors in the west part of the house designed by Bruce, which are panelled, warm, and inviting. This contrast reinforces the impression of Hopetoun as a house of two halves, albeit two halves that sit comfortably side by side and complement each other.

The two distinct interior styles are tied together through the contents and the way they are displayed. Portraits and photographs of various generations of Hopes sit happily amongst furniture that mainly dates from the eighteenth century. As is to be expected, the collection has changed from generation to generation, expanding and, on occasion, contracting. But its core has remained stylistically intact, and more often than not it has been improved upon and added to, a tradition that continues to this day. Where possible, the Hopes have used Scottish craftsmen throughout the house's history. The architects were Scottish; most of the furniture has been made, crafted, or supplied by Scots; and, where possible, paintings (especially the collection of family portraits) have been commissioned from Scottish artists. In terms of Scottish art and architectural history, Hopetoun is considered a national gem. This does not make it parochial or inward looking. That was not within the family's make up; the Hopes have been, overall, liberal-minded unionists, and the house has some fairly cosmopolitan aspects that reflect their interests, from the Dutch trading links of the seventeenth century to the Grand Tourists of the eighteenth. The international diversity of contributors to this book would, one hopes, please the outward-looking, internationally active earlier generations.

Hopetoun is not a stagnant museum: the house and the surrounding landscape form an evolving environment that the family, with the help of advisors and trustees, is attempting to curate carefully and with consideration. It is still very much a home, but one that we are happy to share. The house was designed for show and entertainment, and it is testament to its successful design that it continues to do so with grace. In the chapters that follow, eminent authors write with passion and knowledge about that rare phenomenon: a house that is neither wrapped in cotton wool and tied up with red tape, nor stripped back and redecorated in a purely contemporary or historical way. The interiors of Hopetoun as a family home are, I believe, resoundingly authentic.

The new information that has come to light, combined with expanded historical research and improved surveying technics, has resulted in an insightful study of one of Britain's great houses. I hope you will enjoy it.

I–III The octagonal staircase of the Bruce house

IV   The Garden
      Room

V Detail of the State Bed in the Bruce Bedchamber

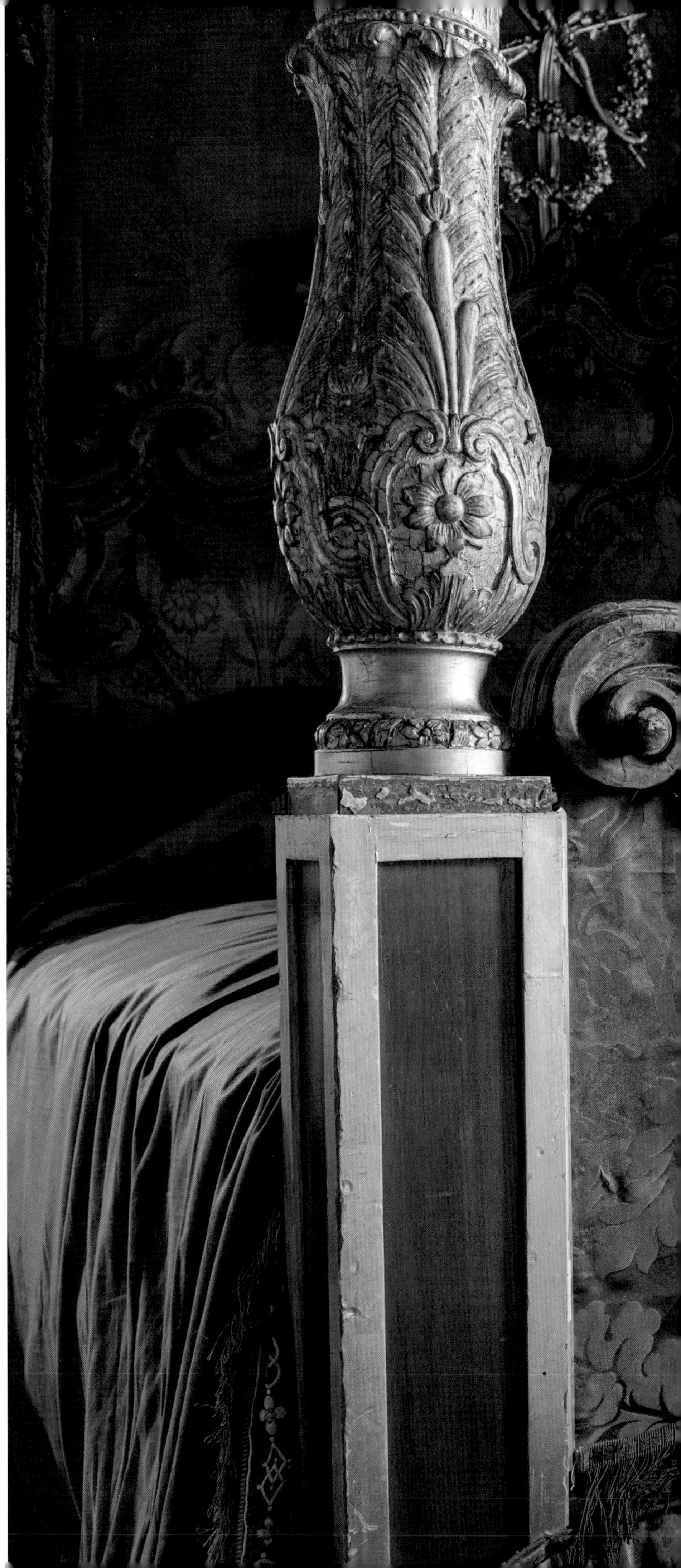

The Hope Family

by Lord Alexander Hope

The history of the Hope family spans more than 500 years of public life in Scotland, Britain, and the British Empire. Members of the dynasty have worked, lived, and served with distinction in an extraordinarily wide range of affairs: legal, political, diplomatic, economic, cultural, clerical, martial, and scientific. The family's origins however, have often been, and still sometimes are, confused. For a long time the family were thought, mistakenly, to be of French or Dutch descent, their earliest antecedent being wrongly identified as 'Jehan de Houblon', who was said to have arrived in Scotland in the train of Madeleine de Valois, the wife of King James V.

The Reformation

The earliest demonstrable ancestor of the family was in fact a Scot, John Hope (c.1475–1554/61), who is recorded in the Edinburgh Burgess Rolls of 1516–17 as 'John [Hope], alias Petit Johne, trumpeter'. He is likely to be the same man who appears in various contemporary entries in the accounts of the Lord High Treasurer, fulfilling a court role of royal herald as well as musician. In time, Petit John established himself as a merchant in Edinburgh and Leith, and was married, firstly to Jane Kirkpatrick and, secondly, to Elizabeth (Bessie) Eumont. In 1533 he became a guild brother of Edinburgh. It is not known how the Houblon/Hope confusion arose, but it seems that, in his heraldic role, Petit John Hope accompanied King James on his 1536 journey to France to meet and marry his new bride, escorting Queen Madeleine back to Scotland the next year. If so, then it is likely that Jehan de Houblon was never more than a translation of John Hope's name, and that no such person ever independently existed.

The date of John Hope's death is unknown, although thought to be between 1554 and 1561. His eldest son by his first marriage was Edward Hope, who achieved prominence as one of the chief supporters of John Knox during the reign of Mary, Queen of Scots. As such, he was chosen as a Commissioner for the Metropolis in the first General Assembly of the Church of Scotland in 1560 and was one of the most fervent of the city's bailiffs acting against any 'massmonger, or obstinate papist, that corrupted the people, suche as preests, friars, and others of that sort, that should be found within the toun'. His religious conviction and political prominence inevitably pitted him against the Queen, and in 1561 she ordered Hope, Adam Fullerton, and Archibald Douglas of Kilspindie, the Provost of Edinburgh, 'to be charged to waird in the Castell, and commanded a new electioun to be made of proveist and bailliffes'. Edward's opposition to the Queen and her supporters continued unabated, and he was subsequently involved as one of the leading Edinburgh burgesses on the Regent's side in the 'Lang Siege' of Edinburgh Castle in 1571.

That determined support for the Presbyterian Church of Scotland was a hallmark of the family at the time. Edward's younger half-brother, Henry (Harry) Hope (1533–c.1591), seems to have incurred the government's ire for similar reasons. In the Records of the Burgh of Edinburgh, an entry of 1586 records that Harry Hoip [sic], Burgess of Dieppe, was exempted from paying a tax on the inhabitants of Edinburgh as 'he is banist for the cause of religion'. It is unclear where Harry's connections with Dieppe began, but he was registered there as a Merchant Burgess in 1586, two years before becoming a burgess and guild brother of Edinburgh in 1588. However, his connections may well have predated those years by some time, as he married Jacqueline de Tot, a Frenchwoman possibly from Dieppe, presumably in c.1570.

The Civil War and Commonwealth

Henry's second son, Thomas, was born in Scotland in 1573. Pursuing a career in the law, and in the absence of his exiled parents, Thomas trained under his kinsman, John Nicolson of Lasswade, whom he much later described as 'my maister, under quhom I learnit not only my calling as a citizen, but my calling as a Christian'.

Admitted to the faculty of advocates in 1605, Hope's first major case was the 1606 treason trial of six Presbyterian ministers who had refused to accept the supremacy of the Scottish Privy Council over the General Assembly of the Church of Scotland. It was so politically charged that when the ministers refused to plead guilty, the two lead advocates withdrew, leaving Hope, assisted by another junior advocate, to plead on their behalf. The case was unwinnable, but Hope's defence was perceived to be of such quality that he established a reputation not only as one of the leading advocates of his generation, but also as a man of remarkable principle: 'the estimatioune both of a guid man and of a guid advocate', as his contemporary James Melville (1556–1614) succinctly commented. It also resulted in Hope becoming the *de facto* legal counsel for the supporters of Scottish Presbyterianism. Consequently, it was perhaps surprising when in 1626, the year after the accession of Charles I, Hope was appointed Lord Advocate *(fig. 1)*, the chief legal officer of the Crown in Scotland and one of the Great Officers of State, and in 1628 was created a baronet as Sir Thomas Hope of Craighall. His advancement should probably be seen in part as the recognition of his legal pre-eminence, but also as an attempt to try to win over a potential opponent through the use of royal patronage. If so, that policy may initially have seemed successful, as Thomas spent much of the first decade of his office reinforcing the Crown's authority and prerogative in Scotland, most notably conducting the 1635 trial against Lord Balmerino. The latter proceedings proved an early watershed in the incipient breach between the King and the supporters of the Church of Scotland, and one might expect from his actions that Hope would be marked as a confirmed supporter of the King's party. In reality, Hope became increasingly associated with the opponents of royal ecclesiastical policy.

Over the next decade, Hope continuously strove to maintain a policy of interpreting the royal prerogative through the circumscription of the law, thereby remaining true to his religious convictions. Perhaps most illustrative of Hope's policy was his approach to the 1638 King's Covenant. He signed it, and worked actively towards its general acceptance, but used his legal knowledge and ability to show it to be exactly the same as the National Covenant, precluding all religious innovations, entirely contrary to the intentions of the King. Hope's actions resulted in the effective obstruction of many of the attempts to enforce the royal will by the Crown's ministers, in the opinion of whom he was treasonably loyal to the Covenanters and Dissenters—the Marquis of Hamilton reserving a particular enmity for him. The fact was, however,

fig. 1
Sir Thomas Hope, Lord Advocate (1573–1646). Drawing by David Steuart Erskine

that on those occasions where the Covenanters acted in direct contravention to the lawful rights of the Crown, Hope stood against them, once explaining to the Earl of Rothes: 'for civill points, luik nevir to haif me to go with yow.' As a result, he only once incurred the King's overt wrath, being banished in 1640 to his house at Craighall, in Fife. Even then—unlike so many of his contemporaries—rather than turn against his monarch, he merely wrote: 'I am to goo to morrow to the place of my confyning And to remayne and die thair, if so be youre majesty's pleasure.'

His banishment proved to be temporary, but Hope's crisis of conscience was a miniature version of that afflicting the whole realm as it descended into civil war. His position at the apex of both royal and religious authority—in 1643 he served as Lord High Commissioner to the General Assembly of the Kirk of Scotland—during the Covenanting crisis was, however, unique. The strain had physical and mental consequences for him, but he never wavered in his sense of duty to both God and King; he died in 1646, and has been remembered as one of the great figures of Scottish legal history. It was in no small part due to his sponsorship and encouragement that Sir Thomas was followed into the law by three of his sons from his marriage to Elizabeth Bennet: Sir John Hope of Craighall (later Lord Craighall), Sir Thomas Hope of Kerse, and Sir James Hope of Hopetoun. All three became judges in the Court of Session during their father's lifetime. On occasion, the Lord Advocate was required to address the Court, and, it being considered unseemly that a father should bare his head before his child, the right was introduced for the Lord Advocate to plead with his head covered: a right that remains attached, albeit unused, to the office to this day.

Of the considerable estates that Sir Thomas acquired in his lifetime, the primary, Craighall in Fife, passed to his eldest son and heir Sir John Hope of Craighall, from whom descend the Hope Baronets of Craighall, the senior branch of the family. It is from the Lord Advocate's youngest son, Sir James Hope, that the Hopes of Hopetoun are descended *(fig. 2)*. In January 1639, James married Anna, the daughter and heiress of the Edinburgh merchant and goldsmith, Robert Foulis. Through her, he became owner of a valuable mining estate in Lanarkshire known as Leadhills *(fig. 3)*, which proved to be critical to the Hope family's fortune over the succeeding centuries. Although Sir James would be known to posterity more for his political than his mercantile endeavours, the latter were extensive, focusing for the most part on the improvement of the lead mines

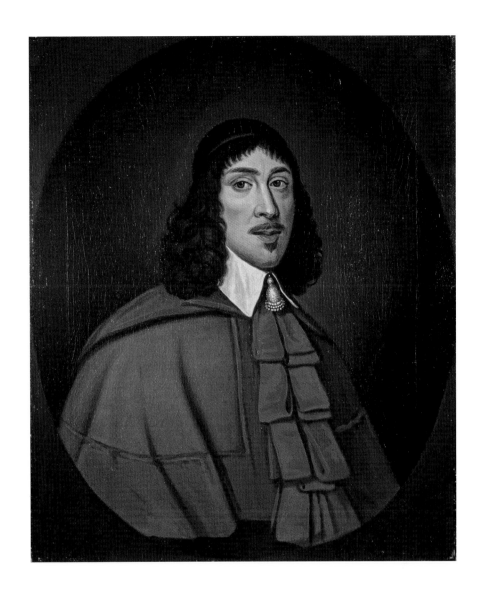

fig. 2
Sir James Hope of Hopetoun (1614–1661). Painting by L. Schuneman

fig. 3
Lead mining at Leadhills.
Watercolour by Paul
Sandby (1751)

and the management of consequent trading links with the continent, particularly the United Provinces. It was doubtless because of his knowledge of mining and smelting that he was made Master of the Mint in 1641.

In the growing civil struggle that so defined his father's career, Sir James maintained the latter's close links with and sympathy for the Covenanting cause, but, unlike him, he held no office that necessitated a division of loyalties. Instead he became increasingly affiliated with radical elements within the Covenanters, a group coloured by an apocalyptic belief that drove its call for political and religious reform. It was with that faction that he sided as a member of the Scottish Whiggamore parliament of 1649; and as one of its leaders, he, with his eldest brother Sir John Hope, Lord Craighall, opposed the 1650 Treaty of Breda with the young King Charles II. Deeply concerned that such opposition would presage war with England, the siblings advised the King and his chief Scottish supporter, the Marquess of Argyll, to come to terms with Cromwell's regime in London—Craighall in 1651 famously advising the young prince 'to treat with Cromwell for the one halff of his cloacke before he lost the quhole'. Their position as foremost statesmen of the radical wing was underlined when, in December of that year, in the aftermath of the Battle of Worcester and Charles II's flight, they held a clandestine meeting at Craighall with two of Cromwell's Major-Generals, Lambert and Deane, and one of the surviving Royalists, John Swinton of Swinton, to discuss the establishment of Commonwealth rule in Scotland.

Given their political prominence, it was no surprise that the Hope brothers became leading figures in Cromwell's various administrative bodies for Scotland and the wider

fig. 4
The wreck of the
Gloucester off Yarmouth,
6 May 1682. Painting by
Johan Danckerts

Commonwealth, including Craighall's appointment as one of the eight commissioners installed to run Scottish affairs, his and Sir James's appointment successively to the Commission of Justice for Scotland, then Sir James's as one of the four Scottish members of the British Barebone's Parliament of 1653 (in which he sat on the crucial committee for legal reform), and lastly as the only Scot on Cromwell's Council of State. The latter appointment, combined with his legal responsibilities in the Commission of Justice and the Parliament, gave Sir James a position that might be compared with the later office of Secretary of State for Scotland. In the execution of his affairs, however, his continuing efforts for reform and the radical nature of his beliefs led to an inevitable fall from political favour: he was not re-elected to the Council, and, after an explosive personal confrontation with Cromwell following the dissolution of the Parliament (when Sir James and his fellow radicals were ejected from the chamber at gunpoint), he was stripped of all offices and retired to his estates.

Disillusioned by the failure of his vision for reform, Sir James returned to Scotland, where he devoted himself to his business affairs, declaring that he had 'no scruple to serve under this or any other power whatsoever in such publict imployment'. However, despite the prominence of his disagreement with Cromwell, his naturally likeable nature seems not to have soured his relationship with the Lord Protector and his government; although, whilst his name periodically came up as a possibility for the Scottish

commission, it was only in March 1660—in the last days of the Protectorate—that he was reappointed to the body, which may not even have assembled by the time of the Restoration a few weeks later. Perhaps it was that relative popularity that explains his escape from political recrimination or even trial after the Restoration. As it was, he died only the next year, 1661, of the epidemic known as the 'Flanders sickness', which he had contracted on a business trip to the United Provinces.

Sir James's principal heir was his eldest surviving son, John Hope of Hopetoun. The latter continued to expand the family estates, crucially purchasing in 1678 the barony of Abercorn in Linlithgowshire, along with the hereditary office of Sheriff of the County. He subsequently added to that the baronies of Niddry and Winchburgh, transferring the family residence to Niddry Castle, and in 1681 was returned as Member of Parliament for the county. It seems that the family escaped any political opprobrium for their prominence in the Commonwealth, as John Hope was close enough to the Duke of York—the future King James II—to travel with him in 1682 on the voyage of HMS *Gloucester* when it was wrecked in the North Sea, losing his life in the disaster *(fig. 4)*.

The Union and Scottish Enlightenment

At his death, John Hope left an only son, Charles, less than a year old, and a daughter, Helen, aged five, with his widow Lady Margaret, daughter of John, fourth Earl of Haddington. Lady Margaret seems to have managed her young son's inheritance and it was she, presumably in consultation with her son, who signed the commission, dated 21 December 1698, for Sir William Bruce to erect a mansion on a promontory jutting into the Firth of Forth on the Barony of Abercorn. Eight months later, on 31 August 1699, her son (now eighteen years of age) *(fig. 5)* married Lady Henrietta Johnstone (1682–1750) *(fig. 6)*, daughter of William, second Earl of Annandale and Hartfell, subsequently first Marquess of Annandale (1664–1721). At his majority, the young laird found himself the owner of rich, unencumbered estates—with only a single sister to support—and son-in-law of one of the nation's foremost peers. The latter connection was of crucial importance: Annandale had held high office, and at the beginning of the eighteenth century was the principal ally of the Earl of Argyll in supporting the governments of the Duke of Queensberry, for which in 1701 he was raised to the marquessate, and Argyll to a dukedom. It is almost certainly a reflection of his influence that his young son-in-law, already hereditary Sheriff of the County, was elected as a parliamentary commissioner for Linlithgowshire in 1702 and on 15 April 1703 was raised to the peerage as Earl of Hopetoun, Viscount Aithrie and Baron Hope, and sworn of the Privy Council. In that capacity he served as one of the key members of the court party in the introduction of the 1707 Act of Union.

fig. 7
Charles Hope-Weir
(1710–1791). Painting by
David Allan

The initial effects of the Union proved, however, to be disappointing, breeding discontent that was to fan the flames of support for the first Jacobite rebellion of 1715. The leaders of that revolt, who had lost their offices on the accession of the Whig-favoured King George I, were for the most part not so much committed adherents of the exiled Stuarts, as Tory supporters of Queen Anne. As a prominent Scottish Whig, and from a family noted for their adherence to Presbyterianism (he was himself to be appointed Lord High Commissioner of the General Assembly of the Church of Scotland in 1723), Hopetoun was firmly opposed to the claims of the Catholic Stuarts in exile. His loyalty during the crisis only enhanced his reputation with the administration and, allied by then with the group of Scottish Whigs supporting John Ker, first Duke of Roxburghe (c.1680–1741), he sat as a Representative Peer from 1722 until his death in 1742. In 1734 he was appointed a Lord of Police, and in 1740 he became Governor of the Bank of Scotland, as well as being invested as a Knight of the Thistle in 1738.

Although the benefits of the Union may have taken longer to appear than had been hoped, in time they did, and by the 1720s lowland Scotland was seeing the first shoots of economic and cultural growth that were to develop by the middle of the century into the full flowering of the Scottish Enlightenment. An early example of this may be seen in Lord Hopetoun's decision in 1721 to commission from a relatively obscure architect, William Adam, the first of a series of works to extend and remodel the east front of Hopetoun. Adam's rebuilding programme would last for twenty-one years,

fig. 8
The third Earl of Hopetoun
(1741–1817) and his family
by the Firth of Forth.
Painting by David Allan

finishing in the year of the Earl's death, and would establish him as the leading Scottish architect of his day. This patronage was not, however, the family's greatest contribution to the architecture of eighteenth-century Britain. That achievement was the suggestion of his son and heir, John, second Earl of Hopetoun (1704–1781) *(fig. 130)* that Adam's young son, Robert (1728–1792), accompany his own younger brother, Charles Hope-Weir *(fig. 7)*, on the latter's Grand Tour in 1754. The two men fell out in Rome, but Adam continued to benefit from Lord Hopetoun's patronage, spending in total five years on his Tour and returning as the master of the classical idiom who would both transform Edinburgh and establish the architectural and decorative style that carries his name. After the completion of the exterior, the second Earl employed Robert and his brother John Adam to decorate the interior of the palace.

The second Earl of Hopetoun's extensive patronage of the arts and sciences reflected his considerable interest in the advances in agriculture and mining made possible by the Industrial and Agricultural Revolutions. He was thereby able to extend the family's estates further as well as to endow such good causes as the Royal Infirmary in Edinburgh, in the establishment and early stages of which he was the primary bene-factor. Besides the Adam family, he was also significant in his early patronage of the young Allan Ramsay, the leading Scottish portraitist of his generation. Ramsay's links with the Hope family date from before his own birth: his grandfather was the Earl's factor at Leadhills, where his father was born, and Lord Hopetoun preserved the connection, becoming an early and enduring patron of the artist.

The Napoleonic Era

On the national stage, however, the second Earl remained largely inactive. In this he was largely followed by his eldest surviving son, James, third Earl of Hopetoun (1741–1816) *(fig. 8)*, who devoted his life to the family's extensive estates in East and West Lothian, Fife and Lanarkshire, including the Annandale estates that he inherited as *de jure* Earl of Annandale on the death of his great-uncle, the third Marquess. That passivity was not, however, followed by the rest of the family, whose careers were fostered by a brother-in-law of the third Earl, Henry Dundas of Arniston, later Viscount Melville. As Pitt the Younger's principal Scottish ally, the latter exercised an extraordinary political hegemony in Scotland during the French Revolutionary and Napoleonic Wars. As members of Dundas's family interest, all the patronage at Dundas's disposal was available to the Hopes, and they repaid this with considerable success, counting amongst their number a naval Post Captain, three Admirals (two serving as Lords of the Admiralty, one also as Lord High Admiral and one of Nelson's Captains at Trafalgar), the Lord Advocate of Scotland, Lord President of the Court of Session and Lord Justice-General, several Members of Parliament, and no fewer than five Generals.

fig. 9
The fourth Earl of Hopetoun (1765–1823). Print after a painting by Henry Raeburn

The most significant of them was the third Earl's younger half-brother, General Sir John Hope (1765–1823), who would later succeed him as fourth Earl *(fig. 9)*. Enlisting in the 10th Light Dragoons in 1784, John Hope rose through various regiments until attaining the rank of Lieutenant-Colonel of the 25th Foot. He served with this regiment as Adjutant-General under Sir Ralph Abercromby in the West Indies in 1796–7, his conduct attracting the commendation of the Commander-in-Chief. Hope became Deputy Adjutant-General of the advance force in the 1799 expedition to the Netherlands, but he was invalided home after a wound to the ankle. He returned later in the year as Adjutant-General under the Duke of York, fighting at the battles of Bergen and Castricum. Continuing with Abercromby to the Mediterranean, he again served at the landing at Aboukir Bay and subsequent battles, despite being wounded again at the Battle of Alexandria (at which his patron, Abercromby, was mortally wounded); he was then promoted to Brigadier-General. Both the surrender of Cairo by the French General Belliard and of Alexandria by General de Menou were negotiated by him.

SIR JOHN HOPE TAKEN PRISONER AT THE SORTIE OF BAYONNE.

London Published by Thomas Kelly Paternoster row, April 1 1815

fig. 10
The capture of General Sir
John Hope, later fourth
Earl of Hopetoun (1765–
1823), at Bayonne in 1814

Promotions to Major-General and Lieutenant-General ensued, and in 1808 he was sent with the expedition to Sweden under the command of Lieutenant-General Sir John Moore, KB (1761–1809). Disagreements with King Gustavus IV resulted in Moore's recall to England—Hope went with him, the two being sent to Portugal, where Moore took command of the British forces in the Peninsula, advancing into Spain with Hope as the commander of one of the two divisions, including all of Moore's artillery and cavalry. Shortly afterwards, Napoleon invaded Portugal with an overwhelming force of 200,000 men, forcing Moore to withdraw his army in the middle of winter, through the mountains and to the port of La Coruña. There, to save the army until it could embark, he organised a defensive position, Hope commanding the left flank. Moore was fatally wounded in the ensuing French attack and Hope took over command. Having held off the French attack, he oversaw the evacuation of the army, personally checking every street to ensure that nobody was left behind. According to dispatches describing the event, to Hope's

fig. 11
The visit of George IV to
Hopetoun in 1822.
Watercolour by Denis
Dighton

'abilities and exertions, in the direction of the ardent zeal and unconquerable valour of his majesty's troops, is to be attributed, under Providence, the success of the day, which terminated in the complete and entire repulse and defeat of the enemy'. For his conduct and gallantry Hope received the thanks of Parliament and was made a Knight of the Bath.

Four years later, in 1813, Sir John returned to the Peninsula, taking over from his cousin, Major-General Sir Thomas Graham. There, he was placed second in seniority, but not in command, to Wellington, leading the 1st division at the Battle of Nivelle, and the 1st, 5th, and Light Divisions at the Battles of the Nive, where he was again wounded. After the crossing of the Adour in 1814, he was engaged in the siege of Bayonne when, in a night sortie on 14 April, he was wounded and briefly captured *(fig. 10)*. The siege was ended by Napoleon's abdication, and Hope was released, but his injury prevented him from serving further on active duty. After the war, he was raised to the peerage in his own right as Baron Niddry of Niddry Castle, although he declined a pecuniary grant offered by Parliament. Two years later, in 1816, he succeeded his elder half-brother as fourth Earl of Hopetoun, and in 1819 was made full General. Not only was he Colonel of the 92nd Gordon Highlanders and then the 42nd Highlanders, and a Knight Grand Cross of the Bath, but also served as Lord-Lieutenant of Linlithgowshire, Gold Stick for Scotland, and Governor of the Royal Bank of Scotland. In 1822, Wellington, in gratitude to the man he once described as 'the ablest man in the Peninsular army', also offered him the position of Lieutenant-General of the Ordinance, but Hopetoun declined the offer, occupied as he was with the management of the family estates.

His responsibilities were considerable, and taken up by the Earl with enthusiasm. Hopetoun House and its immediate policies were in need of care, partly because the third Earl had been in his later years both ill and a widower, and therefore had not given the building the attention that he had been able to devote to it in earlier years. In addition, the proper bequest to his daughter, Jemima (the *de jure* heiress of the Annandale titles, the Annandale estates, and much of her father's collections), meant that the house lost some of its contents (mostly pictures): a shortfall that Hopetoun addressed

fig. 12
The fifth Earl of Hopetoun
(1803–1843). Painting by
Watson Gordon

by engaging the services of the artist and agent Andrew Wilson. The care he dedicated to the house proved to be exceptionally well timed. As one of Scotland's most prominent noblemen and one of its greatest surviving war heroes, Hopetoun was to play a considerable role in the 1822 visit of King George IV to Scotland. Since 1819, Hopetoun had been Captain-General of the Royal Company of Archers, taking a considerable interest in, and helping to revitalise, the institution. Clad in their green tartan uniforms, they were used as an escort in many of the public parades and, over the course of his visit, the King was so struck by the splendour of the Royal Company that he designated it the Royal Bodyguard for Scotland and appointed Lord Hopetoun Gold Stick for Scotland.

Only a few days before the visit, Lord Melville informed Lord Hopetoun that the King wished to visit him at Hopetoun House on the morning of the last day of the tour, lunching with the family and their guests, before sailing south from Port Edgar *(fig. 11)*. Despite such short notice, the event proved a fitting ending to the visit, including as it did the knighting in the saloon of Captain Adam Ferguson, the Keeper of the Regalia of Scotland, and Henry Raeburn, the artist. Sadly, however, Lord Hopetoun did not live to enjoy the honours of his retirement, his constitution having been damaged by the various wounds incurred throughout his military career, and he died suddenly in 1823 on a trip to Paris with his sons, James and Charles. The late Earl's body was brought back to Scotland and was ultimately buried in the family mausoleum at Abercorn *(fig. 41)*, in the park at Hopetoun. Two Hopetoun monuments, on Byres Hill, East Lothian, and Mount Hill, Fife, commemorate him *(fig. 45)*, as does a bronze statue in St. Andrew Square, Edinburgh.

The Victorian Age

At his father's death, James, fifth Earl of Hopetoun, born in 1803, was only nineteen years old, recently graduated from Christ Church, Oxford, and fifteen months short of his majority *(fig. 12)*. Two years later, he married Hon. Louisa Bosville Macdonald (1802–1854), and their only surviving child, John Alexander, was born in 1831. James divided most of his relatively short life between the management of the family estates and participation in the House of Lords. He died suddenly in his carriage on the night of 8 April 1843, on his way home from Parliament.

fig. 13
The sixth Earl of Hopetoun (1831–1873). Painting, circle of Sir Francis Grant

    Five of Lord Hopetoun's brothers reached adulthood and pursued the military and political careers that were the preferred paths of the *cursus honorum* of the British aristocracy of the time. The second son, James (1807–1854), rose to become a Lieutenant-Colonel in the 2nd Foot Guards (Coldstream Guards) and became the M.P. for the family seat of Linlithgowshire from 1835 to 1838, following the retirement of his uncle, General Hon. Sir Alexander Hope. In 1844, he inherited Featherstone Castle, Northumberland, and its estate from his uncle, Lord Wallace, changing his surname to Hope-Wallace. When James vacated his Linlithgowshire seat, it was taken over by his younger brother, Charles (1808–1863), who held it until 1845, when he became Lieutenant Governor of the Isle of Man, staying in that office until 1860. The third brother, George (1811–1854), joined the navy, reaching the rank of Captain before his premature death. Louis (1817–1894) joined the Coldstream Guards before travelling to Australia, where in 1862 he planted 325 acres of sugar cane, becoming one of the founders of the Australian sugar industry, returning to Britain in 1884.

    The youngest of the fifth Earl's brothers, Adrian (1828–1858), joined the army as a Second Lieutenant in the 60th Rifles, fighting in the eighth Xhosa War (Mlanjeni's War) in 1850–3 and the Crimean War in 1854–5. Transferred as a Lieutenant-Colonel to the 93rd (Sutherland) Highlanders in 1855, his regiment were en route to China in 1857 when news reached them of the outbreak of the Indian Mutiny. Diverted to India, Hope commanded the Highland Brigade at the Relief of Lucknow, the Second Battle of Cawnpore, for which he was mentioned in dispatches. Promoted to Brigadier-General, he was killed shortly afterwards in the campaign, on 15 April 1858, by a sniper at the attack on Fort Ruhya. The Sutherland Highlanders killed in the Indian Mutiny are commemorated in a monument in St Giles' Cathedral, Edinburgh; there is also a memorial stone to Brigadier Hope in the west aisle of the north transept of Westminster Abbey.

At much the same time, their cousin, Colonel William Hope (1834–1909), was awarded the Victoria Cross for his actions at the Battle of the Great Redan during the

fig. 14

Inauguration of the seventh Earl of Hopetoun (1860–1908) as Governor-General of Australia, 1901

The Inauguration of the Australian Commonwealth.

Photo. Copyright.

SWEARING IN THE GOVERNOR-GENERAL.

Kerry.

The ceremony took place on January 1 in a pavilion in Centennial Park. This was a handsome structure in pure white, emblazoned with the names of the federating colonies. It was erected in a level hollow in the park, surrounded by rising ground forming a vast amphitheatre, which enabled thousands of people to witness the proceedings. After a special prayer by the Archbishop, Lord Hopetoun took the oath of office, which was the signal for firing a salute, the National Anthem was played by the massed bands, and prolonged cheers were raised.

1855 siege of Sebastopol. His medal, which was one of those presented at the honour's first investiture, is now in the Royal Fusiliers Museum in the Tower of London.

These early deaths and absences overseas left John, sixth Earl of Hopetoun (1831–1873), as heir *(fig. 13)*. There were very few adult male relatives around him in his teens and early adulthood, as even those of his uncles that still lived were not resident in Scotland. It may be partly because of this lack of example that the sixth Earl's life differed radically from those of his ancestors. Rather than politics, the law, or the army, the great passion of Lord Hopetoun's life was field sports. On attaining his majority, he became Master of the Pytchley Hunt in Leicestershire and, although maintaining that role for only four years, retained a connection with the county for the rest of his life. After his marriage in 1860 to Etheldred Anne Birch-Reynardson, they rented a house, Lubenham Hall; then, in 1866, they purchased the nearby Papillon Hall, where the family frequently stayed until its sale shortly before the Earl's death. Although the marriage was a very happy one, much of the rest of the Earl's brief life was spent away from his family, either shooting on the estate at Leadhills, fishing at home and abroad, or visiting the fashionable resorts of Europe. On one such trip, Lord Hopetoun—whose health, like so many of his family, was never strong—caught typhus, dying in Florence on 1 April 1873 at the age of forty-two.

fig. 15
Equestrian statue of the seventh Earl of Hopetoun (later first Marquess of Linlithgow) in Melbourne, by W. Birnie Rhind, unveiled 1911

The Governor-General

For the third generation in a row, therefore, the new Earl was a child: John Adrian Louis, seventh Earl of Hopetoun (1860–1908), was twelve when he inherited the title. From his early maturity it became clear that the course of his life would differ markedly from that of his father. Educated at Eton and the Royal Military College, Sandhurst, he entered public life at an early age, becoming a junior Conservative Whip in the House of Lords in 1883, serving in Lord Salisbury's first and second ministries until 1889, when he was appointed Governor of the state of Victoria, Australia *(fig. 134)*. Possessed of an easy aristocratic charm, an extravagantly generous nature, and an able diplomatic instinct, he proved an ideal tonic in a period of regional financial depression and political instability.

Returning to England in 1895, he served in Lord Salisbury's third ministry as Paymaster-General and then as Lord Chamberlain. Appointed GCMG before leaving for

Victoria in 1889, in 1900 he also became a GCVO and a Knight of the Thistle when he accepted the position of first Governor-General of the newly created Commonwealth of Australia *(fig. 14)*. On the voyage out to Sydney, the Hopetouns disastrously stayed in India, where the Earl was struck down by typhoid, arriving in Australia in a state of physical debilitation. Upon arrival, his main task was to appoint a Prime Minister to form an interim government. Hopetoun was advised by the Chief Justice of New South Wales, Sir Frederick Darley, and the former Prime Minister, Sir George Reid, that correct protocol suggested the appointment should be Sir William Lyne, the Premier of New South Wales, rather than the generally expected candidate, Edmund Barton. Weakened and exhausted by his disease, Hopetoun acceded without questioning this advice. Known as the 'Hopetoun Blunder', the decision may have followed correct protocol but was undoubtedly a diplomatic mistake.

This sort of constitutional haggling, largely occasioned by issues left unresolved by the Federation Bill, became a source of unbearable friction to the Governor-General, who eventually asked to be recalled, returning to Britain in July 1902. Hopetoun's resignation was a cause for regret amongst many who had been greatly attached to him, and the press broadly agreed that Parliament had behaved shabbily. In the end, however, the Governor-General was unable to reconcile his own vision of a unified Australia of the same ceremonial dignity as in India, with the more modest expectations of local politicians. The future Australian premier, Alfred Deakin, provided an insightful epitaph in *The Morning Post* of 2 September 1902: 'Our first Governor-General may be said to have taken with him all the decorations and display and some of the anticipations that splendidly surrounded the inauguration of our national existence … we have … revised our estimate of high office, stripping it too hastily, but not unkindly, of its festal trappings. The stately ceremonial was fitting, but it has been completed' *(fig. 15)*.

Back in Britain, Hopetoun's efforts were recognised when, on 27 October 1902, he was created first Marquess of Linlithgow. But the physical and mental strains of his time in office had cost the new Lord Linlithgow dearly. His health never fully recovered, and

he largely withdrew from public life, although he was persuaded by Arthur Balfour to serve as Secretary of State for Scotland in 1905. The majority of his last years were spent in France for the sake of his health, but there was little that could be done, and he died in 1908, at the Villa Cecil, near Pau, aged just forty-seven. He left behind three children, including his heir, Victor, second Marquess of Linlithgow (1887–1952); a younger son, Lord Charles Hope (1892–1962); and a daughter, Lady Mary Hope (1903–1995), who in 1936 married Sidney Herbert, sixth Earl of Pembroke and thirteenth Earl of Montgomery (1906–1969).

The Viceroy

The diplomatic issues that had faced his father in Australia paled in comparison to those encountered by the second Marquess in his career. Educated, like the Governor-General, at Eton, he embarked at an early age on a political career, before the outbreak of the First World War interrupted all other interests. Serving throughout the conflict —including service on the Western Front—he attained the rank of Colonel in the Lothian and Border Horse, commanding a battalion of the Royal Scots, and was mentioned in dispatches and awarded a military OBE before returning to the political arena *(fig. 16)*. He served in various offices in the 1920s and early 1930s, including that of Civil Lord of the Admiralty and, most importantly for his subsequent life, chairman of the Royal Commission on Agriculture in India (1926–8) and of the Joint Select Committee on Indian Constitutional Reform (1933–4). The latter body was effectively responsible for drafting the Government of India Act of August 1935, the next stage in the progress of

India from directly governed colony to autonomous dominion. Much of the responsibility for the Act's implementation would fall to the successor of the incumbent Viceroy of India, Lord Willingdon, who was due to retire in April 1936, and Linlithgow was the understandable choice to take up the challenge.

His term as Viceroy *(figs. 17, 18, and 135)* was to be the longest of all holders of the office. It was also one of the most complex and intractable. The political arena in India had become so fractious, and the involved parties so mired in mutual mistrust, that Linlithgow faced monumental obstacles to the implementation of local self-government embodied in the 1935 Act designed to create a single, unified constitutional entity before Dominion status was achieved. The Indian National Congress, the largest political grouping of native Indians, wanted immediate independence, and was therefore opposed to any interim stage. Crucially, it also insisted that it represented the sole legitimate voice of native India. That was, inevitably, wholly unacceptable to the subcontinent's minorities—in particular the country's ninety million Muslims—and to the semi-autonomous rulers of the native Princely States. Those groups were alarmed by Congress's position and wanted safeguards for their own rights and cultures in a post-independence nation. For the same reason, a small number within those minorities, particularly the Princes, did not want independence at all. In this they were supported by a reactionary wing of the Conservative Party, notably Churchill, for whom the idea of Indian independence was unacceptable.

Linlithgow disagreed and was in the forefront of those Conservatives who understood that Dominion status, and thereby Independence, was, to his regret, inevitable and should be granted. However, like many, he wanted India to stay within the broad Imperial-Commonwealth framework, and for a substantial British influence to remain in the region. Realising that this was most likely to happen with gradual change, he saw that this was also the only way to protect the unity of the subcontinent, which in the patrician view of India was regarded as a key part of the Imperial legacy. The Viceroy laboured over the next two years to persuade the various parties to agree to the implementation of the Federation.

However, the 1939 onset of the Second World War forced the abandonment of all attempts at constitutional change, although with the intention to recommence them when peace was restored. India's status as an Imperial Colony, rather than a Dominion, meant that it was automatically included in Britain's declaration of war. Not unreasonably, many Indians, and most significantly Congress, felt that it was wholly wrong that therefore not a single Indian was consulted over the subcontinent's commitment. But it is necessary to emphasize that (contrary to wide historical commentary) because of this Linlithgow did *not* declare war on behalf of India without consulting a single Indian. The Viceroy had neither the power to declare war, nor to override the British Government's own declaration. All he was able to do was to relay the British decision, informing India that it, too, was thereby at war with Germany.

Immediately afterwards, and as previously agreed, the Viceroy embarked on an exhaustive series of interviews with all the major political figures in the subcontinent. In his meeting with Gandhi on 4 September 1939, the latter said that, although he could not speak on behalf of Congress, he—despite his personal stance of non-violence—pledged his support for the British cause. He told the Viceroy that he contemplated the war 'with an English heart' and wept at the prospect of bombs falling on Westminster Abbey.

Gandhi's professed view was not echoed by Nehru and the Congress leaders. They saw the war as an opportunity to press their demands for independence on their own terms, demanding a British guarantee of that constitutional separation as a precondition of their cooperation. The British were neither able nor prepared to accept Congress's demands, as the latter were aware, and on 17 October Linlithgow voiced the British response. This was rejected by Congress, and from that moment British cooperation with Congress ceased, and the war was prosecuted in India with the support of the Princely States, the Muslim League, and the non-Congress Hindu population. As the opposition of Congress deepened, the imprisonment of its leaders ensued, culminating in Gandhi's hunger strike in 1943.

In this way, the war provided the opportunity for the leaders of the Indian National Congress to place Britain in a position of constitutional deadlock that could only be broken by complete rupture, leading in 1947 to the partition of India and East and West Pakistan. The tragedy is that partition was the price that Congress paid for Indian independence on the unilateral terms that they had so long espoused and that Linlithgow and the majority of the British administration had so long known to be at odds with reality.

On his return to Britain in 1943, Linlithgow retired from public service, physically worn out by the demands of the office. Offered the choice between a dukedom or Knighthood of the Garter, he chose the latter, which he held along with the Order of the Thistle, the Order of the Indian Empire, the Order of the Star of India, and the Order of the British Empire. He died not long afterwards in 1952, aged sixty-four, whilst shooting at Hopetoun: family tradition holds that he fell dead into his loader's arms. Having two sons, he was succeeded by the eldest, Charles, as third Marquess of Linlithgow. The younger, Lord John Hope, served as a Member of Parliament for Midlothian and Peebles North from 1945 to 1950 and then Edinburgh Pentlands from 1950 to 1964, serving from 1959 to 1962 as Minister for Works. In 1964 he was raised to the peerage as Baron Glendevon, dying in 1996.

Lord Glendevon was not, however, the last member of the wider Hope family to achieve office. Continuing the long tradition of public service, and specifically the family's historic connection with the law in Scotland, in 1989 James Arthur David Hope, a direct descendant of the first Earl, became a Senator of the College of Justice and was appointed Lord President of the Court of Session and Lord Justice-General. Granted a life peerage in 1995 as Lord Hope of Craighead, he retired in 1996, becoming a Lord of Appeal in Ordinary until 2009 when he was appointed Deputy President of the Supreme Court of the United Kingdom and also invested as a Knight of the Thistle. Lord Hope's appointment came 363 years after Sir Thomas Hope was appointed Lord Advocate, the latest in a tradition and continuity of service that would no doubt have given great pleasure to the family's common ancestor.

Overleaf:

VIII / IX In the Library

X / XI Glass pane marked with
its destination room and
uniform box in the attic

XII Boxes in the
Charter Room

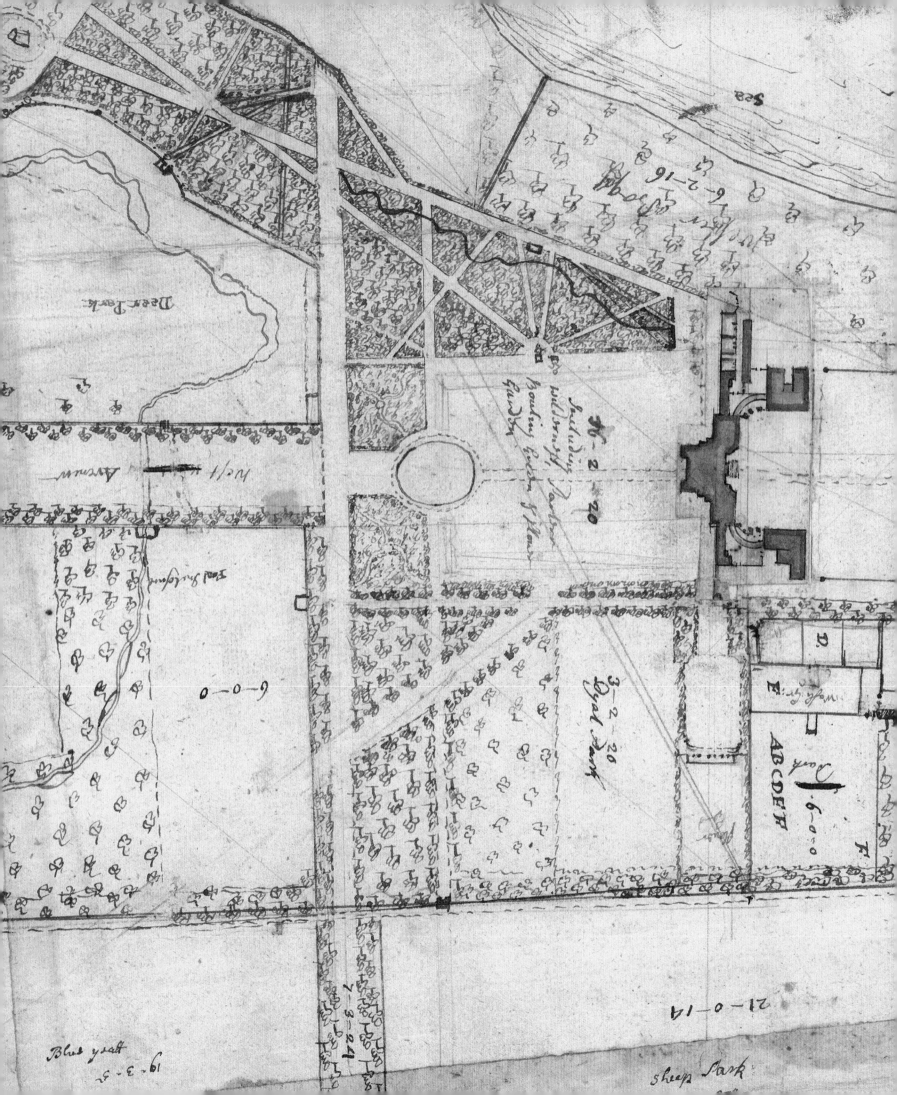

Sea

16 – 2 – 16

Deer Park

16 – 2 – 20

including walks or bowling Green & New Garden

Nell Walk   Avenue

East Bridgend

0 – 0 – 9

3 – 2 – 20
Deer Park

D

Hishfor

E

Park
6 – 0 – 0
ABCDEF

F

21 – 0 – 14

7 – 3 – 24

Blue yeat
19 – 3 – 5

Sheep Park

chapter 2

The Designed Landscape

by Christopher Dingwall

Laying the foundations of today's landscape

A mongst the earliest descriptions of the gardens at Hopetoun House is one written by Sir Robert Sibbald in 1710; this was immediately after the completion of the first part of the new mansion house, which had been designed by Sir William Bruce for Lady Margaret Hamilton and her young son Charles Hope. Sibbald's account speaks of 'a stately house with avenues on all quarters, fine gardens and orchards'. Work on the landscape must have begun several years earlier, with the formation of the 700-metre-long terrace or platform on which the mansion house stands *(fig. 19)*. A major civil engineering work such as this would not have been beyond the means of the Hope family, whose considerable wealth was generated by extensive coal-mining concerns in Lothian and lead-mining interests at Leadhills in South Lanarkshire, and who must have had access to a large labouring workforce.

Even so, the formation of this first landscape must have taken several years. It is interesting to compare John Adair's manuscript map of 1682—on which the old name of Abercorn has been scored out and the name 'Hopton H[ouse]' has been added rather crudely in a different hand—with the printed version of Adair's map dating from 1737, by which time 'Hoptoun' is depicted as a substantial house already surrounded by extensive enclosures and plantations *(fig. 20)*.[1]

In forming the original landscape, Sir William Bruce is understood to have worked with fellow architect and landscape designer Alexander Edward. Bruce also appears to have drawn on his earlier schemes at his own houses at Balcaskie in the 1670s, and at Kinross House in the 1680s, where care was taken to align the houses and their gardens with a distant eye-catcher.

At Hopetoun the primary focus was on North Berwick Law, a conical hill as far as 50 kilometres (30 miles) to the east. It is likely that Bruce's landscape comprised a direct axial approach leading to a walled forecourt overlooked by the east-facing arrival front of the original house. Beyond and to the west of the house were formal gardens, including a grand parterre *(fig. 21)* and round pond or basin, overlooked by the west-facing or garden front of the house. To the south and east of the house was the kitchen

fig. 19
Aerial view of the
grounds at Hopetoun,
looking east, *c*.2010

fig. 20
Detail from John Adair's
map of 1737 showing
'Hoptoun' surrounded by
its designed landscape

garden, straddling the nearby Thunderbolt Burn. The final design of this landscape may have been influenced by Alexander Edward's tour of England and the near Continent made in 1701–2, when he is known to have visited English houses such as Chatsworth and Castle Howard, along with many grand houses in Holland and France.

Early visitors to Hopetoun during the 1720s, such as John Macky (d. 1726) and Daniel Defoe (d. 1731), expressed their admiration. For the widely travelled Macky, the view from the terrace was 'the finest I saw any where; far beyond Frascati, near to Rome, or St. Michael del Bosco, near Bolognia, for variety … There are several vistos from each of the many walks from the parterre.' Other ideas are likely to have come from observations made by the young John Hope, later second Earl of Hopetoun, in the course of his Grand Tour of Europe made in the 1720s, as well as visits made to other houses in Britain; or from books to be found in the library at Hopetoun.

Development and expansion in the eighteenth century

The aggrandisement of the house in the 1730s and 1740s for the second Earl of Hopetoun by the Scottish architect William Adam (1689–1748) was accompanied by significant alterations to William Bruce's landscape. An undated plan signed by Adam, and thought to date from c.1730 (figs. 22 and 23), saw Bruce's walled forecourt swept away, to be replaced by a broad open lawn circumscribed by a stone-lined ha-ha, giving an uninterrupted view of the house. Some of the decorative stonework from this forecourt was very likely incorporated into the arcaded walls which run north and south from the house today. It seems likely, too, that the elaborate parterre to the west of the house was laid down to grass at the same time. Adam also planned greatly extended waterworks, though much of his scheme of canal ponds and cascades was never executed, whether because of the cost or through the lack of an adequate water supply.

Also seen on Adam's plan is the so-called Wilderness, on a spur of land to the north and west of the house, bounded by a long terrace walk overlooking the Firth of Forth, and doubling back along the north side of the Cornie Burn—the word 'wilderness' at this time denoting a formal plantation cut through with criss-crossing rides and vistas. At Hopetoun, one of these vistas linked the new mansion to the site of old Abercorn Castle, which had been demolished in 1703, serving as a symbolic link between the old and the new. The site of the old castle was described on Adam's plan as 'A Mount with a Banck & Ever Green Wilderness round From whence a Prospect of the whole River and Cuntry as Farr as the Eye can Serve; This Mount is Form'd out the Rubbish of the old Castle of Abercorn – Ane Obelisque on this Mount 90 Feet high.' No evidence has been found to tell us if this obelisk ever existed. As in other landscapes of the period, there were other vistas or rides aligned on more distant features such as Blackness Castle to the west and Niddrie Castle to the south.

We are fortunate in having two estate plans of Hopetoun, one by James Jameson from 1747 *(fig. 24)* and another by John Lesslie in 1759 *(fig. 25)*, which can be compared with Adam's earlier plan, revealing the extent to which Adam's proposals had been executed by the middle of the eighteenth century. These in turn can be studied alongside William Roy's *Military Survey of Scotland*, dating from *c*.1755. They all show a landscape dominated by geometrical elements, laid out in the French style, with the house standing at the centre of a broad east–west avenue or vista. They also depict a narrow vista running south-wards from the house towards Staneyhill, incorporating a bowling green, an area now known as the 'Spring Garden' from

fig. 21
The outlines of the formal garden west of the house, laid out around 1700, as they show up in a dry summer

its spectacular display of daffodils. This feature, between the 'Foals Park' and the 'Calves Park', is described by Adam as 'The Boulling Green with Arcade Faceing it. And Green-house behind Faceing a Little Garden on the South.' This garden is marked on Lesslie's plan, with the addition of a narrow strip of planting running next to and parallel with the south wall of the gardens, threaded through with a sinuous path. We know from docu-ments preserved in the archive that exotic trees and shrubs were brought up from London in 1747 to plant in this area, making it an early Scottish example of an informal shrubbery garden, which may have been modelled on similar features seen by the second Earl of Hopetoun on visits to gardens in England.

The latter half of the eighteenth century was a time of change for many country-house landscapes, as geometrical layouts were superseded by a more informal style of planting first introduced by Adam's contemporary William Kent (1685–1748), and subse-quently developed by his successor Lancelot 'Capability' Brown (1716–1783). Whether as a result of deliberate choice, or through the absence of the third and fifth Earls for long periods, Hopetoun escaped the wholesale remodelling which swept away many other formal gardens which were then replaced by newly fashionable parkland landscapes planted with clumps and standard trees. The changes that did occur at Hopetoun were both gradual and less dramatic, a fact remarked on by the English aesthete Rev. William Gilpin, when he visited in 1776. As he observed, 'The old ideas of formality still exist, and have taken full possession of the environs of the house; but

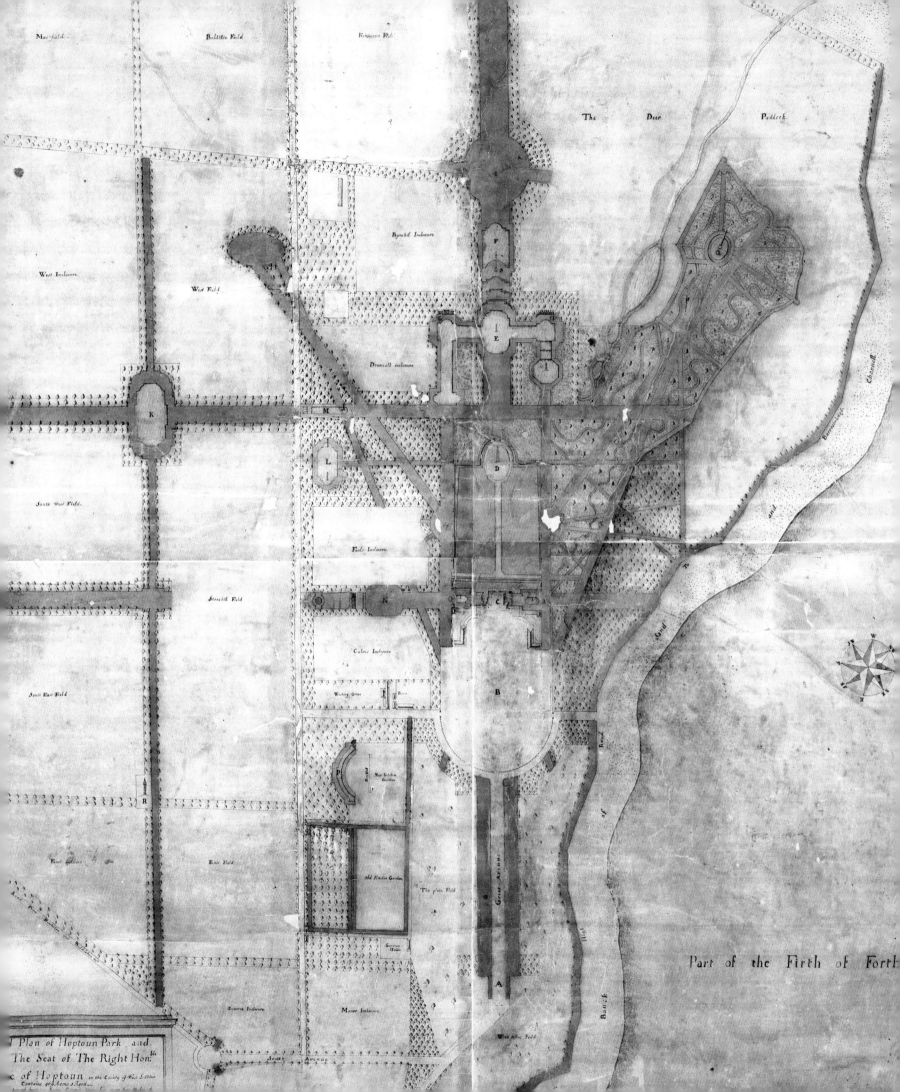

Moss field.

Bohitlic Field.

West Inclosure.

West Field.

Byrehill Inclosure.

The Deer Paddock.

Drumcath inclosure.

Channell

K

South West Field.

L

Foots Inclosure.

D

South East Field.

Stonehill Field.

N

Sand

C

Colzes Inclosure.

B

Road

of

Pond Inclosure.

R

Working Green

New Kitchen Garden

P

East Field.

Bank

Old Kitchen Garden.

The plain Field.

Great Avenue

of

Gardeners House.

A

Part of the Firth of Forth

Avenue Inclosure.

Manr Inclosure.

Wild [...] Field.

South Avenue.

Plan of Hoptoun Park and.
The Seat of The Right Honble
[...] of Hoptoun in the County of West Lothian
[...] Acres [...]

A General Plan of Hoptoun Park and Gardens. The Seat of The Right Hon:ble The Earle of Hoptoun in the County of West Lothian

Contains 469 Acres 1 Rood –

A, *The Avenue Eastward from the House Carries Your Eye over Two Myles of the River Forth to the Island and Ruins of Inchgarvie and from Hence forward along the River 22 Miles more to North Berwick Law. Being a high Mount in Form of a Suggar Loaf, which terminat's the Avenue*

B, *The Court befor the House 774 Feet in Length by 560 Feet in Breadth*

C, *The House Collonads and offices Extending over all 415 1/2 Feet*

D, *A Basson in the Parterre 170 Feet in Length and 120 Feet in Breadth with a jett of 80 Feet High*

E, *A Basson in the West Avenue with a Right Angullar Cannal on each Side. The North Cross Cannal having a Cascade of 3 Falls into ane Octagon Basson.*

F, *A Reservoir above the Cannal abovemention'd in the Line of the Said Avenue, with ane Amphitheatre of Bancks betwixt and the former Basson*

G, *Ane Arcade and Temple Faceing A part of the Cannal & South Walk of Parterre – being Elevated on a rising Ground Commands a view down the River Forth to North Berwick Law*

H, *Ane Avenue of Trellage Work faceing the North Wall of the Parterre and along the River to North Berwick Law*

I, *A Large Circle Upon the Sommet of the Ground in the Avenue Commanding a Prospect of the River Forth and Cuntry on both Sides Eastward to Northberwick Law 24 Miles, and westward to Blackness Castle 2 Miles and forward to Stirling Castle 22 miles more*

K, *A Reservoir of Water From where the Great jett in the Parterre & severall oy:s are supply'd*

L, *A Basson with two jetts*

M, *A Grotto with a Cannal of Watter upon the Levell Ground at the foot of the Banck in the Niddrie Walk.*

N, *The Boulling Green with Arcade Faceing it. And GreenHouse behind Faceing a Little Garden on the South.*

O, *Two Small Bassons and jetts*

P, *A Canal in the Kitchen Garden For Watter Foull*

Q, *A Mount with a Banck & Ever Green Wilderness round From whence a Prospect of the whole River and Cuntry as Farr as the Eye can Serve; This Mount is Form'd out the Rubbish of the old Castle of Abercorn – Ane Obelisque on this Mount 90 Feet high*

R, *The old Tower of Stonehill Upon a Rising Ground*

S, *A Pillar of The Corinthian Order to be done in the Best Manner on which is design't King Georges Statue of a Size Proportion'd to the Height of the Pillar*

Gull. Adam Arch.t Delin t

A General Plan of Hoptoun Park and Gardens. The Seat of The Right Hon:ble The Earle of Hoptoun in the County of West Lothian

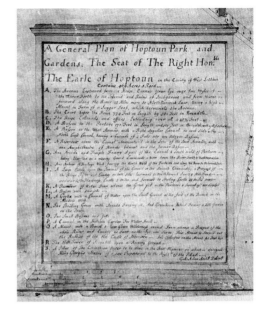

fig. 23
The detailed key to Adam's plan, naming many features, some of which were never executed, such as a Corinthian column bearing a statue of George II

fig. 22
'A General Plan of Hoptoun Park and Gardens. The Seat of The Right Hon:ble The Earle of Hoptoun', by William Adam, *c*.1740

▲ *fig. 24*
Plan of the Hopetoun
landscape by James
Jameson, 1747

► *fig. 25*
'Plan of the Garden
Parks &c. of
Hopetoun House,
by John Lesslie
1759, Partly from
his own surveys
and partly from
those by James
Jameson'

◄ *fig. 26*
A late eighteenth-
century view along
the west front of the
house to the Forth

Plan
Of the Gardens Parks &c
of
Hopetoun House
By John Leslie 1759
Partly from his own Surveys and
partly from those by James Jameson

they might easily be displaced. There is so much depth in the woods, so much variety in the ground, and so much space on every side, that the whole scene is capable of any improvement' *(fig. 26)*.

At the end of the eighteenth century, both the landscape and its landlord were extolled in verse by the Rev. James Cririe in his book *Scottish Scenery: or Sketches in Verse* (1803):

> Fair Hopetoun, seated on a spreading lawn
> In princely state West, North and East enjoys,
> These beauteous, grand, and sweetly vari'd scenes.
> Long, Hopetoun, may'st thou boast thy gen'rous Lord,
> For ev'ry virtue famed, his Country's friend,
> Supremely blest in what his heart delights,
> The great, the godlike powers of doing good,
> From hated schemes of selfish faction free.
> Long may he view, well pleased, thy spreading lawns,
> Thy gently swelling hills and shady groves,
> Thy winding streams and distant mountains high:
> Nor let Italia boast a brighter scene,
> Nor far-fam'd Britain boast a better Lord.

Remodelling in the nineteenth century

The Scottish author and landscape designer John Claudius Loudon visited Hopetoun House in the course of an extensive tour of Scotland made in 1831. His detailed account of the landscape, published not long after in his *Encyclopaedia of Gardening* (1835) together with a plan of the grounds, tells us of further developments which had occurred in the gardens and grounds, mostly under the direction of long-serving gardener James Smith. Loudon, echoing Rev. William Gilpin, commented that 'many changes have been made to bring it closer to the modern taste; but it has never been entirely remodelled. There is still a very extensive lawn, with many right angles and straight lines; but the extreme formality of these lines has been broken, at least to the eye, by the introduction of detached trees.'

Loudon's account goes on to describe the recent and extensive remodelling of the walled gardens, which had involved the installation of new drainage, and the importation of fresh soil. These gardens he described as 'extremely favourable for fruit; the principal of these are apples, pears, apricots and figs, which are produced in great abundance and of excellent quality.' Also noted by Loudon was the recent creation of an arboretum and what he described as an 'American ground, filled with shrubs and other plants which require a moist and peaty soil', together with a 'flower garden stocked with an extensive collection of the most ornamental plants which will stand the open air of

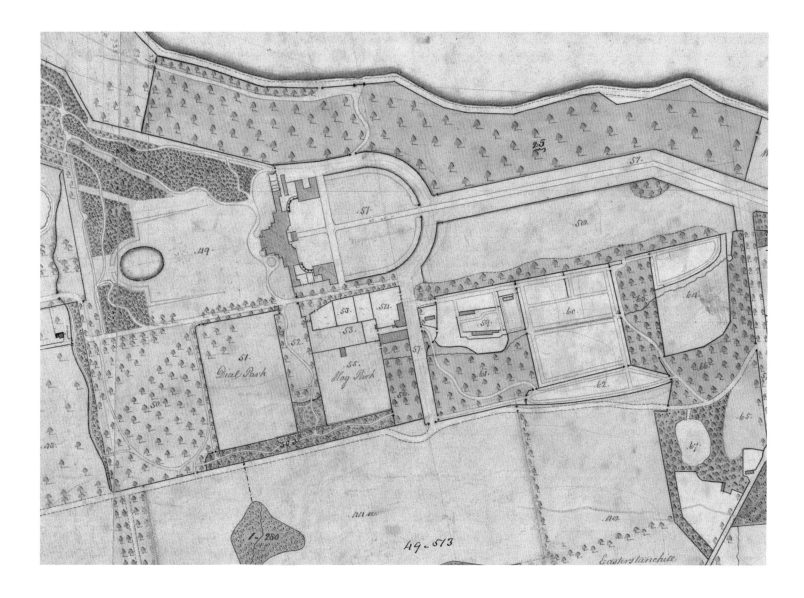

fig. 27
Detail of John Lander's
map of 1815–16 showing the
shrubbery garden south of
the house

this climate'. Amongst the new introductions described by Loudon were rhododen-drons, azaleas, and andromedas, together with showy evergreens *(fig. 27)*.

The latter half of the nineteenth century saw further changes and additions being made to the gardens and grounds, in spite of the fact that both the sixth and the seventh Earl of Hopetoun (later first Marquess of Linlithgow), succeeded to their titles in their minority, aged just twelve and thirteen respectively. By the date of the *First Edition Ordnance Survey* (1854), a new informal path now known as Hope's Walk had been formed in the valley of the Cornie Burn, immediately below the terrace walk surrounding the Wilderness, overlooked by a small semi-circular summerhouse set into the terrace wall. Today's planting in the valley of the Cornie Burn is dominated by rhododendrons, many of which date from the nineteenth-century planting. By the same date, a new alcove known as 'The Pulpit' had been built against the south boundary wall of the garden, near the southern end of the Niddrie cross-axial walk, incorporating stonework from the demolished arcade in the Spring Garden. This feature is now home to a modern sculpture of the figure of Salome by artist John Skelton, commissioned by the third Marquess in 1963. It was under the sixth Earl in *c.*1870 that a new rustic summer house known as the Swiss Cottage was developed, and a nearby bandstand, in Bog Wood, to

fig. 28
Grave marker of Hopetoun's
head gardener James Smith in
the churchyard of Abercorn

the north of the house—sadly both now ruinous and overgrown. Somewhat later in date was the formation of a new eastern approach to the house, with the building of a new entrance and gate lodge in 1895, to a design by R. Rowand Anderson (1834–1921) *(fig. 56)*.

Thanks to the records kept by successive head gardeners such as James Smith (1824–1850) *(fig. 28)* and Adam Niven (1862–1887), and to descriptions of visits made to the gardens, we know a great deal about their management, and the plants being acquired at different times in the nineteenth century. Already, by the mid-century, Hopetoun's gardens were well-known, and widely admired. Records tell of an average of more than 8,000 visitors to the grounds per annum between 1864 and 1870, and of picnic parties using the Staneyhill Park. Francis Groome's *Ordnance Gazetteer of Scotland* (c.1890) described Hopetoun House as 'a stately classical structure ... [with] grounds of singular loveliness—12 acres of garden, laid out like those of Versailles, and a deer park and other policies, whose trees are unrivalled for size and beauty.'

Changes and challenges in the twentieth century

For Hopetoun, as for many other Scottish estates, the twentieth century brought with it many threats and challenges. Changing family and economic circumstances, combined with two World Wars, led to a reduction in the workforce by the middle of the century, with a consequent decline in the management of the gardens and parkland, and the dilapidation or ruination of some built features. Lack of woodland management combined with some less-than-sympathetic coniferous planting led to a parallel decline in the condition of much of the policy woodland. The formation of the Hopetoun House Preservation Trust in 1974, by Charles, third Marquess of Linlithgow, and his son Adrian, has helped to reverse this gradual decline, along with the opening of the house and its grounds to the public on a regular basis. After a period serving as a market garden, the walled gardens were leased to nurseryman Dougal Phillip for some twenty years from the 1970s to the 1990s, before being taken back in hand to be redeveloped as a private garden for the family to enjoy.

With a documented history stretching back more than 400 years, the gardens of Hopetoun have international significance, comparable to that of England's greatest houses such as Blenheim Palace or Castle Howard. As one explores the gardens and grounds today, it is possible to identify elements derived from different periods of their long and complex history and to trace the changes which have occurred. That said, some features have yet to be fully explained and understood. As a result, research into the gardens and their history is ongoing, with a view to answering questions and to

fig. 29
The vista from the house
to the southwest, in the
process of partial renewal

informing future management. Those who care for historic landscapes such as Hopetoun have a difficult line to tread; in the words of Sir Patrick Geddes: 'neither too radically destroying the past in the supposed interest of the present, nor too conservatively allowing the past to limit this, but incorporating the best results of the past with the best we can do in the present, towards the bettering of the opening future' *(fig. 29)*.

chapter 3

Abercorn Church and Churchyard and the Hopetoun Mausoleum

by Peter Burman

W est of Hopetoun House lies the Deer Park and west of the Deer Park lies the estate village of Abercorn whose territory hugs the south bank and foreshore of the mighty River Forth. At the height of the Estate's topographical expansion in the late nineteenth century, it had absorbed a number of smaller estates with their villages and laird's houses. Some of these have been sold off over the years, but the village of Abercorn still belongs to the Estate and is characterized by handsome stone-built houses and cottages and some farm buildings which mostly bear date-stones of the mid-to-late nineteenth century. Characteristically the village-scape is threaded with walls, but they are taller than is usual in Lowland Scottish villages and built of high-quality stone masonry. Abercorn is altogether a special and beautiful place whose full history has yet to be unravelled.

As is common throughout Europe, at the heart of the village is the parish church which sits amidst a large burial ground surrounded by a protective stone wall *(fig. 30)*. Planted with good specimen trees, several dating back to the eighteenth century, it contains grave markers of various forms dating from the seventeenth century up to the present *(fig. 31)*.

The archaeological potential of the church and burial ground at Abercorn is enormous, although largely unexplored. In 1963, an excavation to the north of the church revealed traces of an enclosing *vallum*, or earthen bank, and two small, apparently rectangular structures which may have been monks' quarters within the enclosure. The source of such a plan is ultimately Ireland, but it had already been used in Northumbrian monasteries (for example Whitby, North Yorkshire) and on the island of Iona.

In his *Ecclesiastical History of the English Church and People*, the Venerable Bede, writing in the first quarter of the eighth century, tells how Bishop Trumwine and the monks of the monastery, founded here around 650—an early date for Scotland—were driven out by marauding Picts in 685 after their victory over the Northumbrians at Dunnichen.

What survives of this early period is quite remarkable and consists of the remains of two notable eighth-century stone high crosses of the kind that, particularly in Ireland and in the kingdom of Northumbria, were erected in the churchyards of especially holy

places *(fig. 32)*. The earlier cross has much in common with the celebrated cross of Bewcastle in Cumbria which dates from *c*.670. Its main sides are divided into short panels like the Bewcastle cross and most of the ornament is similar: vine scroll, interlace and a scroll inhabited by beasts and birds, all motifs known to derive ultimately from Mediterranean and Early Christian sources. But there is also a panel of animal interlace, quite unlike anything at Bewcastle. The origin of this form may lie in early metalwork, although similar designs had already been used in the *Lindisfarne Gospels*. The other Abercorn cross can be dated to the later eighth century or possibly even into the early ninth century, on account of the drier and harsher quality of its carving and the presence of a 'ribbon animal'. The human figure does not appear on either cross, in marked contrast to Bewcastle and the still earlier and finer cross at Rothwell in Dumfriesshire. That there were sculptors in eighth-century Lothian capable of competent figure carving is proved by the upper part of an angel preserved on a cross fragment from Aberlady, East Lothian. Yet the most impressive feature of this piece is the panel with intertwined pairs of birds. Its vigour and three-dimensionality are unparalleled by anything earlier than the fantastic twelfth-century trumeaux at Moissac and Beaulieu.

fig. 30
View of Abercorn Church and the churchyard from southeast

fig. 31
Seventeenth-century
grave markers in
Abercorn churchyard

It is worthy of remark that this collection of early carved stones includes two hogback stones and the small fragment of a third. These stones are grave markers with a distinctive curved spine bearing some resemblance to a crouching hog, and they are fairly uncommon. One of them has a fish-scale pattern which imitates roof tiles or shingles and has a steeply rounded back, and the other, which is broken, has longer, irregularly oblong tiles.

Some or all of these carved stone fragments were used as building materials in later centuries and were then rediscovered, most likely at the time of the extensive rebuilding of the church in 1893, when they were disassembled for safe preservation and display. The stones are readily available for study and enjoyment in a small stone structure, originally the Session House, close-panelled inside with pine boarding and a fireplace, near to the entrance to the churchyard.

The main entrance to the church is through a west doorway. It therefore makes sense to begin by describing the church from the northwest and then proceeding anticlockwise to end up with the exceptional early eighteenth-century additions at the

east and north ends. A set of drawings of the church of 1851 survives in the Sime Collection in the archives of Historic Environment Scotland.

The nave of the church was shorter than it is at present, as can be seen by the way the Philpstoun Aisle¹ extends beyond the west wall and even beyond a lean-to porch clipped on to the west wall, with entrances to two separate galleries north and south. On the north side was another burial aisle, marked on one of the 1851 drawings as the 'Duddingston Aisle', approached by external steps laid across its west-facing wall, most likely a private entrance for the family. The presence of a chimney suggests a fireplace— post-Reformation, it was not unusual for the family pew of the laird, or of other notable families, to have a fireplace to keep them warm.

The contrast with the present state is marked. The nave is now almost dwarfed by the north aisle of 1893, which is taller and wider, with a dramatically silhouetted bell-cote over its west gable *(fig. 33)*. There is a central buttress and a pair of round-headed windows with attached columns. The new west termination of the nave is Romanesque in style and given strong emphasis by the doorway having two orders of columns which

fig. 33
Abercorn Church
from northwest

support an entrance archway—the inner order with beakhead and the outer with chevron ornament—framed in a central salient which breaks forward. Over it is a rose window with lavishly carved ornament.

All this new work in the Romanesque manner was designed by a prolific church architect based in Glasgow, Peter Macgregor Chalmers (1859–1922). But why did he choose this style here? Perhaps in emulation of the church of St Cuthbert at Dalmeny on the rival estate of the Earls of Rosebery, three miles to the east. Dalmeny church has been described as 'the best-preserved Norman parish church in the country' (i.e. Scotland). To some extent, Abercorn raises a challenge to it. But an even more compelling explanation is that on the south side of the church is a blocked twelfth-century doorway with a single order of columns and shallow carved chevrons on the arch which encloses a tympanum—one of only two decorated Romanesque tympana in the whole of Scotland. The decoration is modest, a pattern of lozenges lightly scratched into the surface (whereas the other example, at Linton in Roxburghshire, has a figural relief), but nevertheless it is a rarity of which to be proud. Much of the general character of the masonry of the south nave wall suggests that it may also be of the twelfth century.

In the mid-to-late nineteenth century the number of 'seatings' in a church was crucial to its ability to hold as many churchgoers as possible at a time when it was difficult to avoid attending church on Sundays. This is likely to be the reason for adding the north aisle in 1893. But the south side of the church seems altogether more satisfying now that the Philpstoun Aisle of 1727 no longer protrudes past the west wall of the nave. Just to the east of the Philpstoun Aisle is the twelfth-century blocked doorway *(fig. 34)*, clearly delineated in the Sime Collection drawing of 'Abercorn Kirk from the South, Monday 4 August 1851. JS.' This drawing shows that the fabric of the three burial aisles was carefully respected

during the 1893 work. The central burial aisle is taller and grander than the other two and is for members of the Dalyell family of the adjoining estate westwards, the House of the Binns, where the Dalyells still reside. Attached to the chancel is the Duddingston Aisle of 1603, with its distinctive roof covering of large interlocking stone slabs, a rare survival on a parish church *(fig. 35)*.

Viewing the church from the south gives no real hint of the glorious early eighteenth-century addition to the church, the Hopetoun Aisle *(fig. 36)*, held by well-justified family tradition to have been designed by Sir William Bruce (c.1625–1710), architect of the first Hopetoun House—both projects employing the same superlative artist-craftsmen and the classical style. The work was carried out for the first Earl of Hopetoun during 1707–8. Bruce's Hopetoun House was completed in 1708. Bruce's structure was added on to the north side of the chancel, the side from which the Hopetoun family

arrive at the church from the direction of Hopetoun House. On the ground floor is a room designed as the mausoleum or 'cemetery' for the first Earl and his immediate successors. It must have become apparent early on that it was too small to serve for more than a few generations. The recorded burials are of the first three Earls and their Countesses and a few other close family members. The fourth Earl was buried there for about a decade while stock was taken of the situation. The fulfilment of that conversation was the decision to build the Hopetoun Mausoleum. From the entrance door left of the burial chamber a steep staircase leads to the first floor. Going straight ahead the family could, and still do, walk into their 'laird's loft', or private gallery, from which to participate in the service of the Reformed Church and the long sermons. When tired, cold, or hungry they could, unlike their tenants in the church below, retreat to a handsome Retiring Room where a fire would be burning and refreshments would be available. There is also a second Retiring Room, now altered, on the north side of the chancel, also equipped with a fireplace. Architecturally the Hopetoun Aisle presents two façades, one almost continuous with the east wall of the chancel, on which two distinct dates of masonry can be distinguished, and the other on the north side facing towards the Deer Park and ultimately to Hopetoun House. The façades have that most satisfying of characters, two stories in three bays, with harmonious arrangements of windows and doorways.

Inside the chancel, what the worshipper or visitor now sees on the left is the *œil de bœuf* window enabling the family to stay in touch with what was happening in the church from their rooms of retiral; and, since 1893, a head-on view of the gallery where the family could sit in state and listen attentively to the service and to the sermon. Since then, a raised sanctuary has been created in front of the gallery, the communion table placed spanning the lower and upper step, and behind the sanctuary the Hopetoun Aisle is expressed as a panelled front of four tiers, two large and two small rows of panelling. The gallery is deep as well as broad and has a piended ceiling, the west-facing elevation providing a spectacular location for the Earl's coat of arms, the supporters of which are the figures of Hope with their anchors: on either side are vertical garlands of fruits, symbolizing both the fruitfulness of the Hope family line and its smiling prosperity, and two large letters 'H', each surmounted by an Earl's coronet *(fig. 37)*. This vivacious and colourfully painted decoration, rich in heraldic and personal significance for the Hope family, was executed by Richard Waitt in

fig. 37
The Hope coat of arms in the gallery

fig. 38
Grave marker for the Rev Hugh Meiklejohn

fig. 39
Grave marker for
the poet Ian
Hamilton Finlay

1708: it is perfectly complemented by the richly carved openwork valance forming a sort of proscenium arch into the gallery, and by sundry garlanded vertical swags of berries and flowers, all of them invested with a particular meaning. The carvings are all by William Eizat, whose workshop also supplied the elegant joinery for the gallery and Retiring Rooms.

The churchyard or burial ground very clearly appears to be part of the Estate with some notable trees that confirm its character as an extension or special corner of the designed landscape. The enclosing stone wall is as handsome as other stone walls on the estate. The large numbers of grave markers—a useful expression which covers all kinds of monuments or memorials—include many that give the occupation of the deceased, for example 'farmer', 'schoolmaster', or the place where they lived. Notable is the grave marker commemorating one of the longest-serving head gardeners, 'Mr James Smith', whose inscription records that he died 10 February 1850 'in the 74th year of his age and the 60th year of his services under the Earls of Hopetoun' *(fig. 28)*. Notable also are the grave markers of successive factors of the Estate, for example that of William Murray, d. 1847, whose inscription states that it was erected by 'John Alexander Earl of Hopetoun and his curators', curators being an alternative Scots word for trustees. Slightly later, and close to the east end of the Hopetoun Aisle, is the Greek Revival–style pedimented grave marker of 'The Revd Hugh Meiklejohn DD, professor of church history in the University of Edinburgh, Minister of this Parish for forty years…Erected by his parishioners in testimony of their affectionate remembrance' *(fig. 38)*. We note that this is erected by his parishioners, out of affection and esteem, rather than by the Earl of Hopetoun, his principal patron, and that he is celebrated here as Minister not of the church (though of course he was that too) but of the parish, responsible for the pastoral care of all the inhabitants of a large territorial area. It is such a distinguished design that it just might be by William Burn (1789–1870), who had designed the family Mausoleum for the fifth Earl of Hopetoun in 1831, or by his great rival William Henry Playfair (1790–1857), by whom quite a number of recorded monuments are known.

In the southeast corner of the churchyard is the best of the more recent grave markers, by Nicholas Sloan (b. 1951), commemorating the remains of the poet Ian Hamilton Finlay (1925–2006) and his parents *(fig. 39)*. Not only is the lettering superb but each personality is given the tinctured emblem of a daisy, reminding us that Ian Hamilton Finlay designed Little Sparta, considered to be one of the outstanding British garden landscapes of the late twentieth century. Collaborative work by Nicholas Sloan with Ian Hamilton Finlay is to be found in Tate Modern and other European museums and galleries as well as at Little Sparta, where the classical worlds of Ancient Greece and Rome are celebrated: sculpture and fine lettering have an equally important role with the trees, the greensward, and the 'borrowed' landscape beyond.

Churchyards quite often preserve vernacular features which have disappeared from other places. Here, close to the entrance, there is a stile for pedestrians which may also have doubled as a mounting block—apart from the Hopetouns and the other land-owning families, most parishioners would have arrived on foot for services or, from outlying farms, on horseback.

The interior of the church is largely an example of the Romanesque Revival, a grave and serious style which deserves appreciation, especially when carried out with such sophistication as here. The chancel arch and the three-bay arcade of columns and arches between the nave and the north aisle are the most conspicuous features. There is easy access to one of the three burial aisles, namely that of the Dalyells of the House of the Binns; the stone covering to the burial vault with its iron rings can easily be identified. Close to it on the west wall of the aisle are mural tablets of vigorous Baroque character dedicated to Thomas Dalyell (d. 1642) and his wife Janet Bruce (d. 1634). These tablets carry much of the conventional *memento mori* iconography deployed from the late sixteenth century onwards: skulls with crossed bones, hour glasses, mattocks or spades, *putti* blowing trumpets, angels with downturned extinguished torches, and their respective heraldic achievements *(fig. 40)*. The inscription 'Here rest the remanes of Janet Bruce, wife of Thomas Dalyel of Binns' reminds us that a wife's descent from noble forebears was also important to noble families, while Thomas is recorded as being 'descended of the auncient race of the Los [Lords] of Dalyel now Erles of Carnwath' and in a graceful phrase 'efter 69 yeeres pilgrimage on earth hee was removed to the rest of heaven'. It is possible that closer examination of these tablets might produce a signature and that they form part of a corpus of provincial Baroque sculpture.

fig. 41
The Mausoleum
by William Burn,
erected 1833

82

Quite close to Abercorn Church, in the direction of the Deer Park and Hopetoun House, is the family Mausoleum, quite properly a very private place and not readily visible from public paths *(fig. 41)*. It stands in a 1950s memorial garden enclosed by stone walls and entrance gates of wrought ironwork close in character to those at the north end of Hopetoun House sometimes known as the 'Bruce Gates', as this ironwork may well be contemporary with the work of Sir William Bruce. The Mausoleum was designed by William Burn (1789–1870) in 1831–2, and the contract drawings with their precise specifications survive in the Hopetoun Archives. Burn was the son of Robert Burn of Edinburgh, a builder and architect, and was sent to London to become a pupil in Robert Smirke's office from 1808 to 1811. 'By 1830 he had a bigger practice than any other Scottish architect, and could count among his clients the Dukes of Hamilton and Buccleuch, the Earls of Haddington and Kinnoull, and many other influential persons, especially of the Tory party.'

The three contract drawings are headed 'Hopetoun Cemetery' Numbers 1, 2, and 3 respectively, issuing from William Burn's office at 131 George Street, Edinburgh, on 11 December 1832. The building is small, concentrated, and powerful. The style is round-arched but the windows with their simple but elegant bifurcated tracery suggest the influence of Northern Italy. The ground plan consists of an eastern entrance porch, a larger vessel and a smaller vessel, somewhat like a nave and chancel. The 'nave' has two projections on both north and south sides, presumably intended for sarcophagi, while the chancel appears to be a place for burial and commemoration of the most prominent members of the family. The four projections of the nave plan are expressed externally as though they were short stubby transepts, and at the upper level they contain the windows within triangular pediments which also add interest to the roof. The roof, which is drawn out in full, is covered with overlapping stone tiles which recall quite closely those on the Duddingston Aisle of the parish church. On the drawing it states: 'The roof stones to be entirely droved, cheeked 2 inches on each other, and sett and pointed with oil putty. The ridge stones will be polished.' The steps of the entrance porch were also directed to be polished, as was the central walkway of the nave, marked as being of 'polished Arbroath pavements', but the chancel was not to be paved, presumably to allow for burials. Moreover, 'The projecting doorpiece, the mouldings, coping of gables, base course, windows, and decorations will be entirely polished, and the remaining portion of the exterior will be completed with tooled ashlar, having the joints also lipped and pointed with oil putty, made to the colour of the stone.' This first drawing has been endorsed by a different hand, that of the Hopetoun Estate factor at that time, Walter Gowans, with the words, 'Hopetoun House 22 April 1833. This is the Ground plan of the Cemetery to be built in the Park here referred to in the Letter of Obligation to execute the excavation and was on works of the same subscribed by me of this date.'

The second drawing *(fig. 42)* shows the entrance front and one of the two identical side elevations, enriched at every angle by small but beautifully carved animals whose purpose appears to be to ward off evil and protect those buried within. The instructions deal in great detail with the construction of the entrance door and its iron and

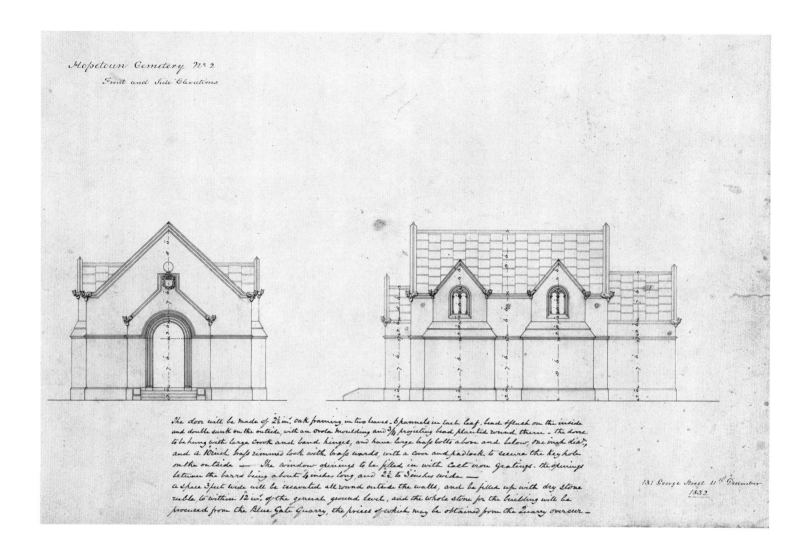

Hopetoun Cemetery No 2.
Front and Side Elevations

The door will be made of 2½ in. oak framing, in two leaves, 6 pannels in each leaf, bead & flush on the inside and double sunk on the outside, with an ovolo moulding and ¾ projecting bead planted round there – the door to be hung with large crook and band hinges, and have large bass bolts above and below, one inch diam, and a Winck brass rimmed lock with brass wards, with a cover and padlock to secure the key hole on the outside – The window openings to be filled in with cast iron Gratings, the openings between the barrs being about 4 inches long, and 2½ to 3 inches wide –
a space 3 feet wide will be excavated all round outside the walls, and be filled up with dry stone ruble, to within 12 in. of the general ground level, and the whole stone for the building will be procured from the Blue Gate Quarry, the prices of which may be obtained from the Quarry overseer –

131 George Street 11th December
1832

fig. 42
Elevations of 'Hopetoun
Cemetery' (the Mausoleum)
by William Burn, dated 1832

brasswork, the cast iron gratings to be supplied for the windows, and 'A space 3 feet wide will be excavated all round outside the walls, and be filled up with dry stone ruble [Scots], to within 12' of the general ground level, and the whole stone for the building will be procured from the Blue Gate Quarry, the prices of which may be obtained from the Quarry overseer.'

The third drawing *(fig. 43)* shows two sections, one being taken at the entrance to the chancel and the other through one of the long sides, showing also that the foundations would be 13 feet 6 inches below the level of the floor. 'The area of the building will be excavated to the levels shown on this section, and until a safe and solid bearing is obtained for the walls, and the inside space on each side of sleeper walls will afterwards be filled up with fine mould or earth to the levels of paved passageway, and between sleeper walls, to within 6 inches of the pavement, and the remaining portion of the excavations will be removed to such place as will be pointed out to contractors.'

Howard Colvin lists more than forty church-related commissions by William Burn, of which the best known are the elegant church of St John, Princes Street, Edinburgh, of 1816–18; the extensive reworking of the exterior facades of the High Kirk of St Giles, Edinburgh, between 1829 and 1833 (close in date to the conception and building of the

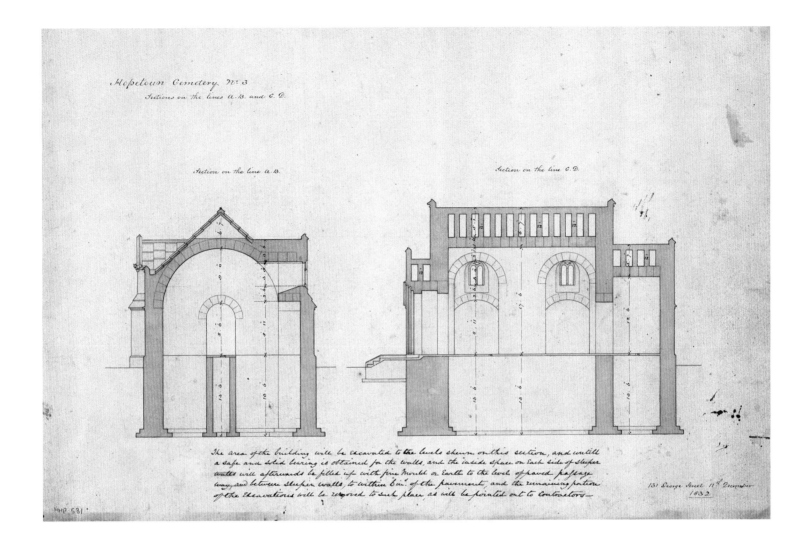

Hopetoun Cemetery. No. 3
Sections on the lines A.B. and C.D.

Section on the line A.B.

Section on the line C.D.

The area of the building will be excavated to the levels shewn on this section, and untill a safe and solid bearing is obtained for the walls, and the inside space on each side of sleeper walls will afterwards be filled up with fine mould or earth to the level of paved passage way, and between sleeper walls, to within 6 in: of the pavement, and the remaining portion of the excavations will be removed to such place, as will be pointed out to contractors—

131 George Street 11th December 1832

HMP 531

fig. 43
Sections of the
Mausoleum by
William Burn

Hopetoun Mausoleum); and the major external restoration of the Rosslyn Chapel from 1837 to *c*.1845. In short, Burn was far and away the most celebrated and prolific designer and restorer of sacred buildings in Scotland during the last half century of his professional practice. Colvin also lists a small number of monuments or mausolea, including the Gothic monument to Burn's father in the Old Calton Burying Ground, Edinburgh (1816); the Melville Monument in St Andrew Square, Edinburgh (1821); mausolea at Killearnadale Kirk, Argyll (for Colin Campbell, 1831); Staindrop Churchyard, Co. Durham (for the second Duke of Cleveland, 1850); Roehampton (for S. Lyne Stephens, 1863-4); and the Packe Family Mausoleum at Branksome Park Estate, Bournemouth (for C.W. Packe, 1867-9)—a remarkable range of achievements, demonstrating a knack for being able to respond to the specific demands of a patron.

Set against this extensive background, the Hopetoun Mausoleum completed in 1833 appears as a smaller work in terms of scale, but of concentrated and thoughtful design and faultless execution. Mercifully it survived the vagaries of fashion and a serious proposal for its demolition in 1953, which went as far as obtaining alternative estimates. Today it can be appreciated and celebrated as a minor masterpiece by a great architect.[2]

chapter 4

The Useful and the Beautiful on the Hopetoun Estate

by Peter Burman

From the late seventeenth century onwards, conscientious landowners throughout Europe have been driven by the idea that they should embrace both 'the useful and the beautiful' on their estates, and Hopetoun is no exception. There is an aspiration that any addition to existing patrimony should be done through good design and with high-quality materials. New buildings have been designed to work well within their historic context, and there has been a willingness to complement buildings and gardens with beautiful works of art commissioned from living artists.

Before taxation took its heavy toll, it was common for noble and other wealthy families to own more than one estate. In the case of Hopetoun, the Estate Yard and the Estate Office would have been creating or commissioning work not only for the Hopetoun Estate but also for the Rankeillor Estate in Fife, the Ormiston Estate in East Lothian, and the Leadhills Estate in Lanarkshire. It is no great surprise, therefore, that we find in the archives of the Hopetoun Archives Trust, preserved at Hopetoun House, plans and architectural drawings for a new Town House at Bathgate *(fig. 44)*, or a new parish church at Ormiston. Surviving plans are legion for housing estate employees and tenants, for farmhouses and farm steadings, for schools and even an inn at Kirkliston. There was also an extensive industrial aspect to the estates, especially at Hopetoun and at Leadhills, which generated the need for specific structures.

The tenants were so appreciative of the fourth Earl's care for their well-being that, after his death in 1823, they raised substantial contributions for the construction of a 'Hopetoun Column' on both the Ormiston and Rankeillor Estates. These columns *(fig. 45)* survive to this day as prominent and much-appreciated landmarks, and still provide spectacular focal points from which to view the landscape. They are also examples of good design and fine craftsmanship.

The fourth Earl (1765–1823) had been a distinguished soldier and a commander in the Peninsular War under the Duke of Wellington *(figs. 9 and 10)*. On inheriting the Earldom and on taking up management of the Estate, he did his best to provide opportunities for local employment. One consequence of this, as we can see and appreciate at Hopetoun, was the construction of stone walls round the perimeter of the core Estate *(fig. 46)*, and the 'sea wall' along the south bank of the River Forth. The stone

Overleaf
Detail of the
main gateway,
from the east

88

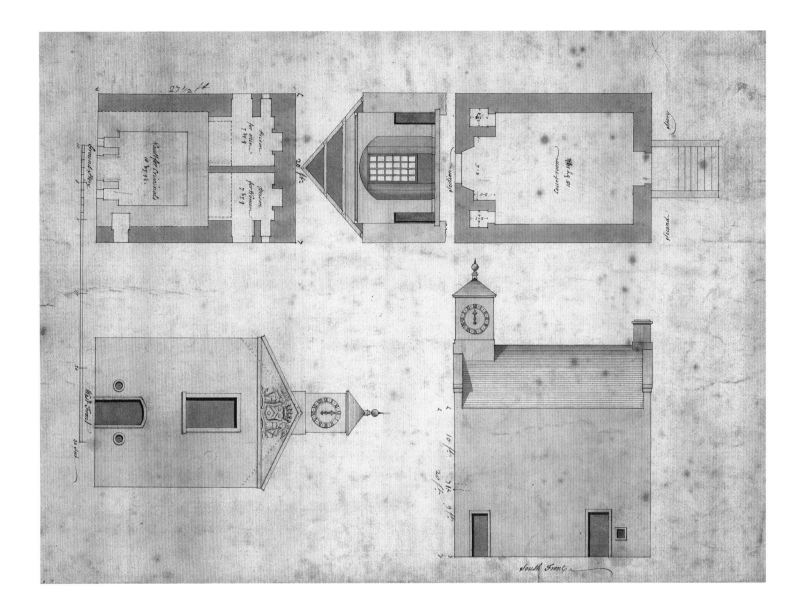

walls around the west and north Deer Parks at Hopetoun are of fundamental importance to the good management of the Estate. They are useful but they are also beautiful and well crafted, and they carry the patina of almost two hundred years. An especially fine visual experience is to walk along the boldly-curving wall between Blue Gate Lodge and the estate village of Abercorn.

Towards the end of the fourth Earl's time there was clearly a feeling that a rural estate needed 'sign-posting' in some way, along with better security and competent people living in gate-lodges to manage the working of the gates. No doubt these gatekeepers kept an observant and shrewd eye on who was coming into and going out of the Estate. Such lodges can be seen throughout the British countryside and they have several functions: they are visual landmarks, showing the existence of an estate with both public and private entrances; they are often architecturally pleasing, some-times designed by the same architect as that of the 'big house' or of other estate buildings; and they provided pleasant living accommodation. The traditional lodge has often been added onto, perhaps in stages, as people's ideas about comfort and security, about bathrooms and kitchens, and about privacy, developed.

fig. 44
Design for a Town House in Bathgate with courtroom and prison

The Hopetoun Archives furnish several designs for lodges. For the Crawstane Lodge (now known as Mid Lodge) there is a 'Specification for Building Crawstane Lodge' dated March 1823 *(figs. 48 and 49)*. It is fascinating to see that the fifth Earl was concerned with the detail of its construction, and the drawings conclude with the following: 'Lord Hopetoun will furnish the Lime, Sand, and Stones and drive the Carriages [i.e. provide the transport]. The Pavement for the Kitchen and such Bricks as may be necessary.' Presumably the contractor provided everything else—essentially the timber for the joinery of the 'common furniture', the floors, stairs, panelling, cupboards, and shelves.

Equally fundamental were the gate-piers of an estate. The Hopetoun Estate needed a significant number of gate-piers both at the perimeter and at various points within the grounds. Every estate tended to develop its own characteristic form of gate-piers (and indeed of gates) and a drawing of 1823 shows the form which is most often encountered at Hopetoun *(fig. 47)*. It is captioned 'The West Gate—Hopetoun House—1823' and is signed by 'J. Scott', most likely someone in the Estate Office, perhaps a building surveyor. The design is for the characteristic 'Humpty Dumpty' round-topped stone piers—an inner and an outer pair—which occur in various locations, and as one pair or two. If you see them you know that you are on Hopetoun territory.

A more ambitious pair of gate-piers is represented by the Obelisk Gateway. The drawing is headed 'Elevation of the Gateway designed at the head of the Cross Avenue' *(fig. 50)*. The location is significant because the visitor walking up the 'Cross Avenue', an avenue of trees through the south parkland, would be drawn forwards by the picturesque and unusual composition of the gateway. The drawing shows an elevation and, below, a 'plan of the Pedestals and Piramides', the latter being a splendidly esoteric alternative to the word 'obelisk'. The proposed gates look modest and as though intended to be made of wood. However, either the gates were not provided in that form or were later replaced by wrought-iron gates on the top of which is a row of finials, oak leaves alternating with exotic flowers *(fig. 51)*. These, or at least the finials, are believed to have formed sections of the screen around the courtyard on the east side of Sir William Bruce's Hopetoun House of 1699–1708. Other sections are incorporated into the 'Bruce Gates', at the extreme north end of Hopetoun House, and as part of the fence surrounding the William Burn Hopetoun Mausoleum of 1831–3.

fig. 45
The Hopetoun
Monument in the
Garleton Hills

fig. 46
A section of
stone wall
within the park

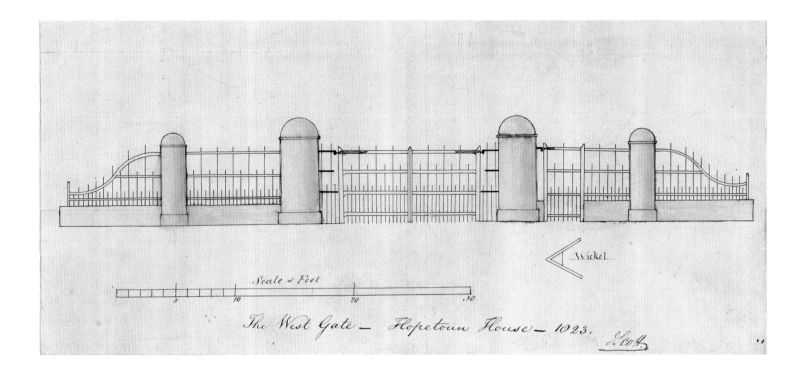

Scale of Feet

The West Gate — Hopetoun House — 1823.   Scott

fig. 47
Drawing for the
West Gate

The finials show the virtuosity of an outstanding artist blacksmith, just as the carvings of Grinling Gibbons (at Hampton Court Palace, say, or St Paul's Cathedral) show what a woodcarver can do at the top of their bent.

One of the most striking of the smaller buildings on the Estate is the Thatched Cottage—a rare survival in Scotland and especially in West Lothian—which today makes an admirable small dwelling *(fig. 52)*. Its strong rustication and the vigorous character of the Baroque window surrounds suggest a date of about 1740. No drawing for it survives. But what was its original purpose? It is strategically placed near the Obelisk Gates, but not adjoining them as would usually be the case for a lodge. Perhaps it housed an estate servant with a particular role which required them to be living more or less out in the landscape, a gamekeeper for example. Or perhaps it housed, or sometimes housed, a hermit? There was quite a fashion for keeping a hermit during the long eighteenth century. For almost three centuries, the Thatched Cottage would have been more isolated than it is now, because the nearby Obelisk Cottages date from the late nineteenth century. They look to belong to the same early Arts and Crafts character as the Parkhead Cottages, or the equally handsome terrace at Woodend, dated 1879 *(fig. 53)*.

At the other end of the scale are the buildings which collectively formed the Home Farm and housed the administrative headquarters of the Estate *(fig. 54)*. This group of buildings is a few minutes' walk from the main house and so easily accessible for successive generations of Earls of Hopetoun. Interestingly, they are not all of one period. The Archives show that there have been many schemes for improving and adding to them, including two plans by James Craig (1739–1795), designer of the plan for the New Town of Edinburgh (1767), an architect whose works are only gradually coming to light. They are beautiful drawings with a strong, confident signature on one of them, including captions showing the intended use of the different spaces. Some less competent nineteenth- and twentieth-century buildings (useful enough in their day) have recently been

fig. 48
The Mid Lodge

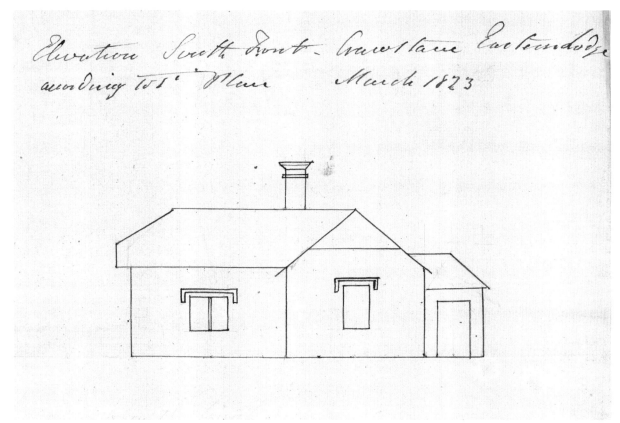

fig. 49
Sketch for
the Mid Lodge

Elevation South Front - Crawstane Eastern lodge
according to 1st Plan   March 1823

demolished. But what survives is of great interest, starting with the former Estate Abattoir of c.1770, converted into a smart Rackets Court around 1900, perfect for country house weekends. Nearby is a kind of funnel, stone-sided, which enabled the animals to be driven to their fate. This building is currently used for light storage but has more than once suggested itself as a future Archives and Research Centre for the Estate.

Closest to Staneyhill Avenue are two large stone buildings of the 1770s. One has been an Estate Workshop, for some decades a Joiners' Workshop, and has been stylishly repurposed by Annie Macpherson of Gray Macpherson Architects as the present Estate Office, a new role which it fulfils admirably. Parallel to it is an even larger building, what appears to be a granary above with cart sheds below, displaying a keystone which declares that it was constructed by 'John Earl of Hopetoun 1774'. It is a handsome building—the useful and the beautiful again— and deserves a new use which would honour and celebrate its scale and craftsmanship while at the same time providing a beneficial income stream to the Estate. The challenge, as always in such cases, is to justify the capital to pay for a repurposing which would necessarily have to be done to a high standard.

On the east side of the new Estate Office is a long low building of c.1840, with a walled garden of its own, which served as the Estate Office well within living memory.

On the west side is a group of buildings which includes Kennels Cottage, the buildings old and new which house the Biomass Plant and its storage of materials, and beyond to the west a range of kennels for hunting dogs, now long out of service but capable of beneficial use as, for example, an adjunct to the Archives, an exhibition gallery, a shop, or a supply room.

A category of building within the Estate which must surely be mentioned is the 'larger' house for specific uses. There is the Garden House which has been skilfully added on to and is now a private residence but was once the home of a series of outstanding Head Gardeners and their families. There is Society House, virtually a small

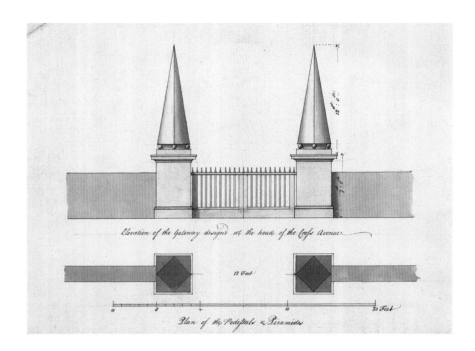

fig. 50
Drawing for the
Obelisk Gateway

fig. 51
Detail of the
Obelisk Gateway

fig. 52
The Thatched
Cottage

fig. 53
Woodend Cottages,
dated 1879

fig. 54
A former Estate
Workshop from
the 1770s, now the
Estate Office

country house with its own tiny hamlet on the south bank of the Forth; it was remodelled as a house of real interest and quality by David Bryce, who was successively a pupil, then partner, of William Burn (architect of the Hopetoun Mausoleum).

To the south of the great Walled Garden, up a steep hill, lies Staneyhill Tower *(fig. 55)*, one of the gentry houses of the several estates taken into the Hopetoun Estate in the late seventeenth and eighteenth centuries, when the Hope family were continuing to grow in wealth and confidently amassing a large estate, creating a property that has largely stood the test of time. What we see is of extraordinary importance: an early seventeenth-century tower house, with vertical strapwork ornament at the corners, and between the strapwork rough rubble stonework which was surely harled originally; and two immense stone-vaulted rooms of great magnificence, perhaps partly medieval, supporting the tower. The tower formerly had a wing on one side, which would have made it an L-plan house.

A complete inventory and survey of all those buildings on the Estate which are plainly of architectural or historic interest would be a considerable undertaking but immensely worthwhile. Such a study could also embrace those buildings which had formerly been part of the Estate but no longer are—for example the austere tower house called Niddry Castle where the first Earl spent his childhood years nurtured by his widowed mother, Lady Margaret Hope.

Finally, we must mention the structure which is for many visitors their first encounter with the Hopetoun Estate and which suggests the splendours within it. It is the tall main entrance Gateway, near the Estate's eastern extremity, close to the river

fig. 55
Staneyhill Tower, the ruin of a seventeenth-century tower house in the park, southeast of the house

shore and not far from Society *(fig. 56)*. It forms an outstanding group with the classical lodge that is just inside the Estate, presenting itself with pediment and columns as though it were a small temple. This is a tripartite structure with stone walls and decorative wrought-iron screenwork and gates with a central overthrow displaying the coat-of-arms of the seventh Earl and the date, 1893.

There is a sequence of links between William Burn (1789–1870), his pupil and successor David Bryce (1803–1876), and Bryce's later partner for a while, the Arts and Crafts architect Sir Robert Rowand Anderson (1834–1921), whose masterpiece is the house called Mount Stuart, built for the third Marquess of Bute. It is deeply satisfying that all three should be present on the Estate, each with a worthwhile example of their high skill as architects—respectively, of the Mausoleum, Society House, and the entrance Gateway and screen.

The Gateway ensemble is designed and executed with real panache. It is a highly effective piece of theatre, like a scene in a courtly masque, or like one of those ceremonial structures which were put up to welcome monarchs or noblemen into cities or displayed on particularly auspicious occasions. It is an architectural flourish worthy of the great house and its estate to which it serves as the welcoming overture.

fig. 56
The main gateway and its lodge, built 1893, seen from inside the Estate

XIII–XV The Yellow
Drawing Room

chapter 5

The House and Its Rooms

by Anne Bantelmann-Betz,
Asita Farnusch, and Leo Schmidt

➤ *fig. 57*
Hopetoun, the view
from the east onto the
façade designed and
built in the 1720s by the
first Earl of Hopetoun
and William Adam

➤ *fig. 58*
Hopetoun seen from
the west: the central
part is the house
designed by Sir William
Bruce just before 1700

Some great houses in Britain were built to one coherent design and have escaped any serious change to their original structure and appearance, but they are few in number. Many resemble Hopetoun in having evolved throughout their history, producing layered composites of interventions—sometimes with unintended results.

At Hopetoun,[1] two phases are clearly visible: the western aspect of the building is dominated by the compact central element of the house built to the design of Sir William Bruce, begun in 1699; whereas the spreading eastern front, designed and built from 1720 onwards by William Adam, exhibits a completely different character. One side appears modest and serious—the other extrovert and triumphant *(figs. 57 and 58)*.

One can try and dissect such a building and look at the 'Bruce house' and the 'Adam house' as separate entities, discussing their specific characteristics and concentrating on their respective architects' intentions, thus seeing the building concepts primarily as autonomous works of art. Or one can focus on the driving force that is more relevant to architecture than to any other form of art: the patron as the owner, inhabitant, and paymaster who wants a house that reflects his wishes and his vision. More accurately we should even take into consideration a *sequence* of owners, each of whom doubtless reflected on the current situation, the state of the building with its perceived drawbacks, and the problems of adapting it to the needs and ambitions of the present. In this approach, a building may be seen as a long, continuous process of communication between generations of owners; each intervention can be read as a comment on the past whilst embodying the values of the present. There would have been two more parameters important for any intervention: the existing building structure (seen partly as an asset and partly as a problem) and the financial means available for the new work.

The first house, circa 1700

Overleaf
Detail of Hopetoun's
east façade

The story of the building of Hopetoun starts long before the first stone was actually laid. In 1678, John Hope bought the two baronies of Niddry and Abercorn situated alongside

fig. 59
Niddry Castle

the Firth of Forth—doubtless with the intention of building a family seat appropriate to his considerable wealth, standing, and ambitions. John was then twenty-eight years of age and married to Lady Margaret Hamilton, daughter of the fourth Earl of Haddington. They had a daughter, Helen, and in 1681 their only son Charles was born. Then tragedy struck. On 6 May 1682, John Hope died in the wreck of the frigate *Gloucester* when travelling with the Duke of York (later King James II) and John Churchill (later Duke of Marlborough). The young family had just moved into Niddry Castle, a vernacular Scots tower house a few miles south of present-day Hopetoun *(fig. 59)*. Mother, son and daughter were to live there for nearly twenty years, but it seems that Lady Margaret and Charles did not lose sight of the idea of building a new house at the earliest possible opportunity.

That time came just before the turn of the century. A detailed agreement with the mason Bachope in 1698 provides the first firm date relating to the building of Hopetoun. Charles Hope was seventeen at the time and it is usually assumed, not unreasonably, that his mother had taken matters into her own hands. But perhaps the son—who later showed himself perfectly capable of dealing with architectural matters—already played a significant part in the conception of the new house. The building project should not be seen in isolation: in view of the fact that Charles was married the following year to Lady Henrietta Johnstone, daughter of the Earl of Annandale and Hartfell, it may be that the Earl and his daughter had insisted, in the negotiations preceding the union, that a decent house was to be built for the new family.

Sir William Bruce *(fig. 60)*, a distant kinsman of the Hopes, was commissioned to build the new house. At the time of the wedding he was just completing Craigiehall (1694–9) for Annandale, and many of the workmen were now available to work at Hopetoun.

It was a shrewd move to create a house of this size and quality, and we assume it was motivated by more than a desire for a spacious new family home. Apart from its qualities as a residence (no doubt greatly appreciated by Charles after growing up in the old, dark tower of Niddry Castle), a house of this ilk, combined with a bride whose background and connections would boost any political ambition, was an excellent springboard for social advancement. It appears to have worked: by 1703, with the house nearing completion, Charles—twenty-two at the time—was created Earl of Hopetoun. In 1705, the family was at last able to take possession. Moving from Niddry Castle into the spacious and well-lit Hopetoun must have felt like a new age.

Erected on practically virgin soil (although nearby Abercorn Castle was demolished and its stones reused for the foundation), the house was named for the family who have lived in it for more than 300 years. It seems likely that the two allegorical figures of Hope on top of the colonnades flanking the main block, with their anchors and orbs, were part of the same concept. This would make them the sole survivors of the seven statues shown atop the Bruce façade when Colen Campbell published the house in the second volume of *Vitruvius Britannicus*, in 1717.

His engravings of a plan and a façade *(fig. 61)* show a well-ordered classical house with pavilions and colonnades. The layout of the main building followed a pattern familiar since Palladio's Villa Capra, better known as *La Rotonda*. Twenty years earlier, the same pattern had been used for the Château de Marly, and, twenty years later, Lord Burlington was to use it at Chiswick. Less pedantic about issues of proportion and symmetry, Bruce's Hopetoun shared the underlying idea of a Greek cross within a square and a domed space in the centre rising through the height of the building. At Hopetoun, this space—narrower than usual for the type—houses an octagonal staircase lit from above. The Entrance Hall and the Garden Parlour lay along the central axis and small apartments filled three of the corner areas; the fourth was used for the Dining Room. Campbell provides no plan of the upper floor but says it had four more apartments and a 'noble Salon' above the Hall.

According to the *Vitruvius Britannicus* plans, there were additional bedrooms in the straight wings stretching north and south, but it would be rash to accept the published scheme as reliable documentation. Opinions are divided as to whether both the impressive corner pavilions and the unusual convex colonnade (characterising the spreading east front of the house) ever existed in this shape, as documents regarding their erection or demolition are scarce and ambiguous. But the central block of the house was undoubtedly built as shown *(fig. 62)*; the façade followed a well-tried classical pattern with a pedimented three-bay centrepiece flanked by two more bays on either side, the basement and two main floors 'rusticated in the *French* manner', as Campbell writes. One hesitates to characterise it as Palladian: with its muted, rather relaxed use of classical motifs, it is rooted in the seventeenth century and is certainly not Palladian in the sense of Inigo Jones, let alone the far more rigorous interpretation of Ancient Rome favoured later by Lord Burlington and his friends.

fig. 60
Sir William Bruce (*c.*1630–1710), portrayed in 1664 by John Michael Wright

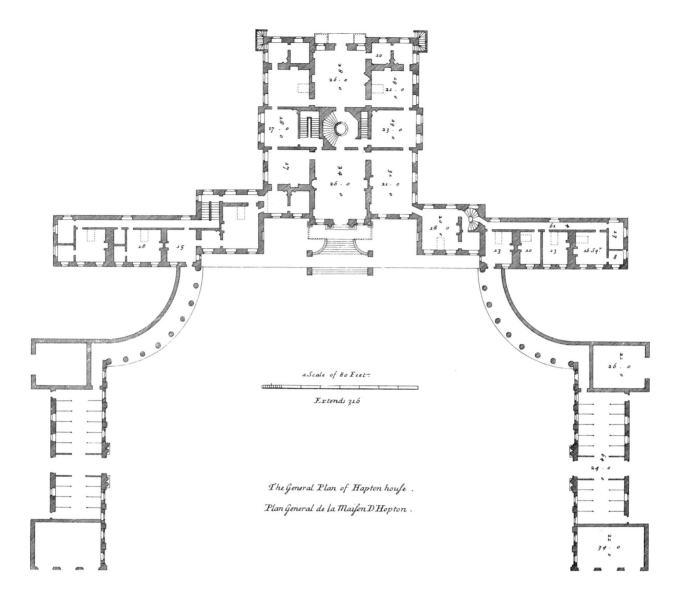

a Scale of 80 Feet.

Extends 316

The General Plan of Hopton house .

Plan General de la Maison D'Hopton .

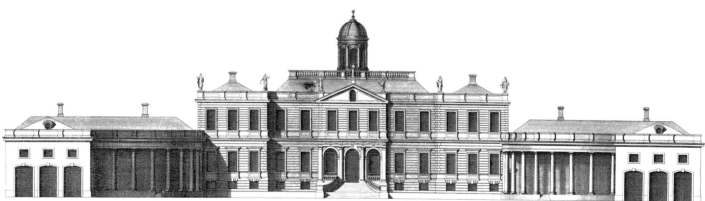

80 Feet   Extends 316

The Elevation of the East Front of Hoptone house in the Shire of Linlithgow in Scotland the Seat of the R.t Hon.ble the Earl of Hoptone
to whom this Plate is most humbly Inscrib'd . Invented by S.r W.m Bruce 1700 .

Elevation Orientale de la Maison D'Hoptone dans le Comte de Linlithgow en Ecosse .

Co: Campbell Delin   H. Hulsbergh Sculp

Kinross, Sir William Bruce's own house, is often mentioned as a model for Hopetoun, but in spite of some similarities there are important differences *(fig. 63)*. Kinross is heavy and massive and somewhat horizontal whereas Hopetoun is more vertical and dynamic in character—not least because of its pediment and spire. Bruce doubtless understood the principle of *convenance*, a term referring less to convenience in the modern sense of the word than to propriety. Whilst Kinross was suitable for a middle-aged gentleman architect, Hopetoun was suitable for a wealthy, well-connected young man intent on making his way. As indeed he did: in the troubled decades following the Act of Union in 1707 and the Jacobite rebellion of 1715, Charles chose the side that ultimately had the upper hand, becoming a prominent Scottish Whig and holding high office, and his descendants followed suit.

◄ *fig. 61*
Plan and elevation of Sir William Bruce's Hopetoun, published in *Vitruvius Britannicus*, vol. II

The grand new scheme of the 1720s

Though perfectly adequate, even sumptuous, at the time of its conception and construction around 1700, the house designed and executed by Bruce had begun to look somewhat dated by the time it was published in the second volume of *Vitruvius Britannicus*. Simultaneously, the house was proving less and less able to cater for the needs of the Earl and his family; between 1704 and 1723, for example, Lady Hopetoun gave birth to thirteen children, nine of whom reached adulthood. Every room of the house and the adjoining ranges must have been filled, obstructing the use of space for one of the important functions of a country house: hosting and entertaining visitors. The point of having a great house in the country was to be on a circuit where members of the country's political and social elite could meet, enjoy themselves, and transact business. But Hopetoun House simply did not have the space for this, at a time when the Earl was keen to advance his career. Nor were its public rooms up to the expected standard.

In retrospect, as James Macaulay has pointed out, publication of the Bruce house in *Vitruvius Britannicus* was an indication of what was afoot. Hopetoun House appeared in it presumably less as a paragon of the qualities Colen Campbell was promoting and more as an attempt by the Scottish architect to attract Lord Hopetoun's patronage and perhaps even a commission for rebuilding the house. Lord Hopetoun, like many of his equals, particularly in England, was not slow to change, embarking on a programme to update the house to his requirements. Need for space as well as continuing political ambitions seem to have motivated him to undertake an extensive building programme.

As architect, Lord Hopetoun chose William Adam *(fig. 64)*, a young builder who had just landed the commission to build Floors Castle for the Duke of Roxburghe. Adam, born in 1689, had been 'bred a Mason and served time as such'.[2] A look at Floors Castle published in *Vitruvius Scoticus (fig. 65)* proves two things: Adam knew how to build a large house, but he had little talent for architectural design.[3] Both those qualities made him the perfect choice for Lord Hopetoun: this was an age when, in Britain, patrons

▲ *fig. 62*
The Bruce house
seen from
northwest—William
Adam's additions
faithfully imitate
the original design

➤ *fig. 63*
Sir William Bruce's
own house,
Kinross, built from
1685 onwards

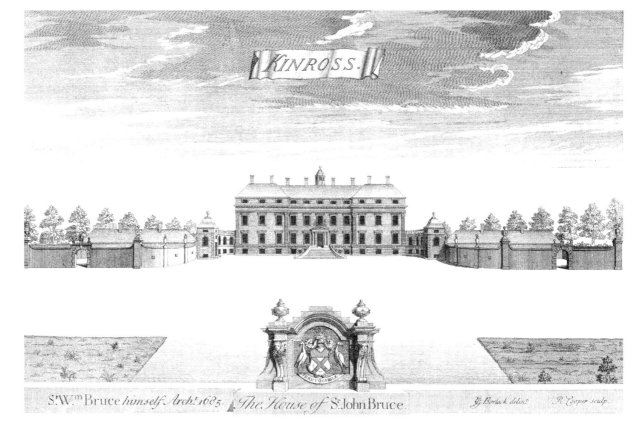

KINROSS.

Sr Wm Bruce *himself. Arch.^t 1685.* The House of Sr John Bruce   G. Borlach delin.^t   R. Cooper sculp.

frequently knew more about buildings—how they should look and how they should work—than their 'architects' did. They were members of the elite who had been steeped in classical culture, had visited Rome, were deeply interested in architecture and its social role, visited each other's houses, and discussed the merits and demerits of external designs and internal arrangements. Architects—unless they were gentlemen like Sir William Bruce—usually came from bricklayers' or masons' families, often displaying amazing technical and organisational skills, but having only a smattering of architectural know-how. In a society with few talented and experienced architects capable of designing large country houses from scratch, connoisseurs like Lord Hopetoun often found able practitioners to carry out their own schemes.[4]

fig. 64
William Adam
(1689–1748), a bust
by Henry Cheere

Using existing and published elevations and plans of ancient Roman buildings and their decoration (such as Antoine Desgodetz's much-perused volume *Edifices antiques de Rome*, published in 1682) was a perfectly respectable way to design a new house. For the design of the new east front, Lord Hopetoun—as Colin McWilliam has convincingly pointed out[5]—took his cue from another house published in *Vitruvius Britannicus*. The centre of Hopetoun's façade, minus the rustication, is clearly lifted from the Marquess of Powis's great town house in Ormond Street in London *(fig. 66)*. It is amazing how quickly things developed. Old Powis House burnt down in January 1713, was built anew in 1714 to the design of an unknown architect and in 1715 Colen Campbell published it in his first volume of *Vitruvius Britannicus*.

To transform this copy of Powis House into a proper country house, a tetrastyle temple front was to be grafted onto the central axis *(figs. 67–69)*, although this, as we shall see, was never actually carried out. Furthermore, the nine-bay town house design was given more breadth and depth by adding three-bay projections at each end. With their corner pilasters, they recall those of Sir William Bruce's own Kinross House. Distinguished by their round-headed windows, they are connected to the centre by a curved section of the façade *(fig. 70)*. Sir John Vanbrugh's Castle Howard and Blenheim Palace as well as Nicholas Hawksmoor's Easton Neston—all published in *Vitruvius Britannicus* and therefore in Lord Hopetoun's mind's eye—lurk in the background of these details. The whole front was thus spread out over an impressive nineteen bays, extended by the effect of colonnades flanking the forecourt.

Building started in the spring of 1722, although no consistent overall concept can possibly have existed at that point, beyond the idea of a grand new east façade. It should be noted that no similar makeover was contemplated for the other side. For the extension to both sides of the central block in the rear or west façade, Lord Hopetoun was happy simply to copy Sir William Bruce's façade so faithfully that the new work

The North Front of Floors Castle toward the Court one of the Seats of His Grace the Duke of Roxbrugh
In the County of Tiviotdale

Gul Adam inv: et delin:

R: Cooper Sculp

▲ *fig. 65*

Floors Castle, the Duke
of Roxburghe's house,
designed by William
Adam and built from 1721
onwards, from *Vitruvius
Scoticus*

cannot be distinguished from the old.[6] The new additions kept to the same floor levels
as the old structure, allowing as far as possible for the integration of the existing parts.

Being able to name sources for the various components of the design should not
detract from the fact that the overall result is both original and successful: in 1723, John
Macky, visiting the construction site, judged that the house 'when finished, will be by
much the finest Seat in Britain'.[7] And it should perhaps be said that, whilst copying
existing designs may be frowned upon today, it was perfectly acceptable in eighteenth-
century Britain. Imitating successful and admired buildings was not only seen, as Oscar
Wilde said much later, as 'the sincerest form of flattery'—it was by far the safest course
in a society which boasted few talented and experienced architects.

A version of the scheme for Hopetoun was published very much later in *Vitruvius
Scoticus*[8] *(figs. 67 and 69)*, using plates that had been engraved from about 1727 onwards,
on the basis of early and even more grandiose concepts. In some respects the published
designs are inconsistent, showing different versions of the concept. The plan of the
ambitious new scheme also features prominently in a portrait of the first Earl, now in the
State Dining Room *(fig. 128)*, but as this was posthumously commissioned by the third
Earl, it has little value as documentary evidence. It can, though, be seen as a sign of the
new incumbent's reverence for his grandfather, who had started the rebuilding of
Hopetoun that had only just been completed on the third Earl's accession in 1781.

Over the next years, the building programme proceeded step by step, with the
sequence of activities illustrating the Earl's priorities. The most pressing issue was
residential space; an addition to the south side of the house—the family area—topped
the list. For reasons of symmetry, the design for the east façade was immutably fixed
with this first new section, although its centre-piece did not become an issue for another
thirty years.

This first element of William Adam's grand new scheme gave the house a lopsided
aspect that could only be tolerated as an intermediate stage for a few years *(fig. 71a)*;

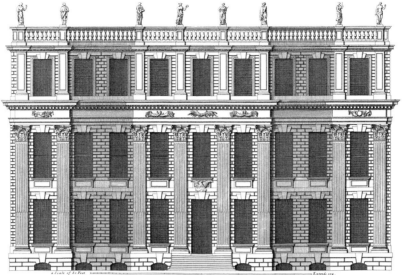

The Elevation of POWIS House in Ormond Street LONDON 1714. Is most humbly Inscrib'd to his Grace the Duke of POWIS &c

Co. Campbell Delin.

Elevation Del. Hostel De POWIS a LONDRES Bati 1714.

◄ *fig. 66*
fig. 66
The elevation of
Powis House in
London, published
in *Vitruvius
Britannicus*, vol. II

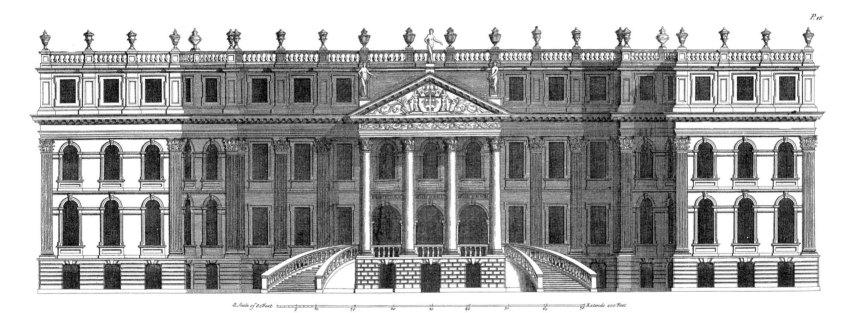

P. 16

A Scale of 80 Feet

The East Front of Hopton House toward the Court

Gull Adams Inr. op delin

R. Cooper Sculp

▲ *fig. 67*
The east front of
Hopetoun House,
as published in
William Adam's
Vitruvius Scoticus

fig. 68
The east front of
Hopetoun House
today

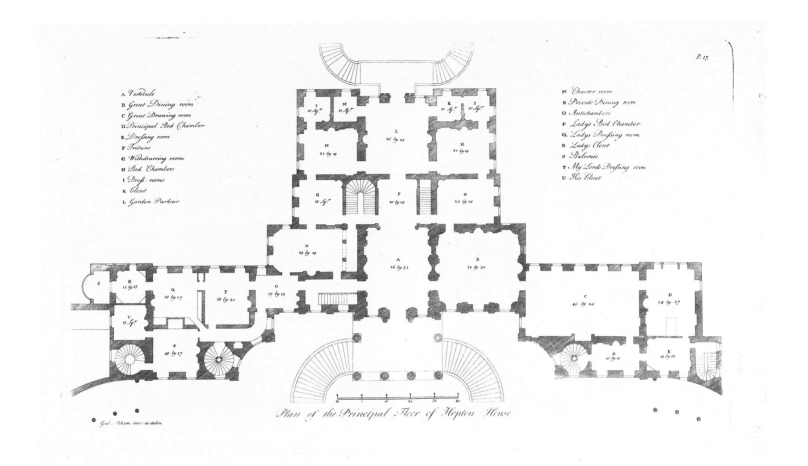

A Vestibule
B Great Dining room
C Great Drawing room
D Principal Bed Chamber
E Dressing room
F Tribune
G Withdrawing rooms
H Bed Chambers
I Dress: rooms
K Closet
L Garden Parlour

M Charter room
N Private Dining room
O Antichambers
P Lady's Bed Chamber
Q Lady's Dressing room
R Lady's Closet
S Balconic
T My Lord's Dressing room
U His Closet

Plan of the Principal Floor of Hopton House

Gul: Adam invt: et delin

fig. 69
Plan of the main floor of Hopetoun House, as published in *Vitruvius Scoticus*

however, the new section immediately increased the space available for the family. At the southern end of the plan of the principal floor we find Lord and Lady Hopetoun's closets as well as a circular backstair giving access to 'My Lord's Dressing Room'. Remarkably, these rooms, though quite important, are not part of the grand new front since they are within a low boxlike addition hidden behind the colonnade. Perhaps this was to afford a measure of privacy, but it also shows a curious disconnection between inside and outside.

Hitherto, the plan of the house and its façade had been pretty much in unison, but now we can see the beginnings of an approach that was to inform the later stages of development and which, over time, led to ever greater discrepancies between the interior organisation of the house and its exterior aspect.

As the impressive new concept initially consisted only of the façade and some general—but in some respects overly grand—ideas for the interior, it lacked a clear vision of the three-dimensional spaces needed. Retaining the floor levels of the Bruce house for the new scheme proved to be a strategic mistake. Further building stages were subsequently planned and executed *ad hoc (fig. 71)*. Without a detailed and realistic scheme at the beginning, unforeseen problems were bound to emerge.

According to the contract with William Adam, this first addition should have been completed within the year, by 1 April 1722, but as the new mason's work was only measured in 1725 it appears that the construction had dragged on somewhat longer than anticipated. A breathing space of three years followed before the Earl again entered into

115

fig. 70
A detail of the east
façade showing the
curved element

a similar agreement with Adam, in February 1728, this time for the erection of the north-ern addition. Remarkably, this agreement stipulated that this was to be two feet longer than the one to the south. No true Palladian would have allowed such a disparity: clearly the Earl and his architect were not driven by exact proportions or precise symmetry. The agreement for the northern extension included enlarging the existing Dining Room, which thus became the first in the sequence of grand reception rooms that were to fill this new space. These rooms, conceived very much like a baroque state apartment, were to culminate in the Principal Bed Chamber at the northern end—again, a room that is prominent in the plan but sits less comfortably from the outside.

Upon completion of the northern addition, a mezzanine was added to the central block to close the unsightly gap in the middle of the façade. Inevitably, the mezzanine clashed with the central tower that was now partly hidden—an unsatisfactory situation that existed for a few years until the tower was removed in 1739.

The 1720s and 1730s also saw the planning and erection of the colonnades and pavilions flanking the great courtyard that opened up towards the grand approach from Edinburgh. The design for the pavilions underwent some changes in shape and function during the process. The long stable fronts to the courtyard shown in *Vitruvius Scoticus* shrank to a more manageable size. With their handsome pedimented seven-bay fronts, both to the courtyard and to the east, the pavilions, each topped by a clock tower, appear as square blocks although they are in fact L-shaped in plan *(figs. 72 and 73)*.

The south pavilion is of particular interest because of the use found for it. Lady Hopetoun's brother, the second Marquess of Annandale, had spent most of his adult life in Italy, acquiring numerous antiquities, works of art, and books. Unmarried and childless, he had made provisions to find a proper home for his treasured possessions. On his death in 1730, many of his assets including his art collection went to his sister rather than to his half-brother. Whereas Annandale's works of art were welcome for furnishing the new rooms at Hopetoun, his books needed a proper library. The south pavilion was chosen for this purpose. Intriguingly, there are designs for the interior of this vast new library inscribed in Italian but giving the measurements both in *Palmi Romani* and in *Piedi Inglese (fig. 74)*. Clearly they were made in Rome for Hopetoun, commissioned there in all likelihood by Lord Annandale himself. The Italian designer may well have worked on the basis of the dimensions given in the drawings of the pavilion's rough construction that also survive in the archives. The library's interior was never completed and the books were instead housed in the mezzanine above the State Apartment which became known as the Annandale rooms. They remained there until the fourth Earl of Hopetoun created a suite of libraries in the Bruce rooms after he inherited in 1816.

Completing and consolidating the house

When the first Earl of Hopetoun died in 1742 he had spent most of his adult life on a construction site. He had watched his house being built first by William Bruce, then reshaped and extended with the able assistance of William Adam. At the time of the accession of the second Earl, the outside of the house already looked pretty much as it does today, apart from the centre of its east façade. The interior, however, was a different matter entirely. The old Bruce house in the centre had changed little in structure, though some rooms had been modernised by the time of the first Earl's death. The dining room off the Entrance Hall, enlarged between 1728 and 1731, was still an empty shell, as were the spaces beyond, within the northern extension. The new Earl, John, was thirty-eight when he inherited, and had two baby boys: it would have been quite natural for him to embark immediately on the task of completing the house. But the 1740s were difficult years, culminating in the Battle of Culloden, and it was not until 1748 that Lord Hopetoun decided to start a new phase of building.

In 1748, William Adam died. His tomb in Greyfriars Kirkyard in Edinburgh features, within a sarcophagus-shaped frame, a relief showing, on the left side, a view along the northwest pavilion of Hopetoun looking towards a Palladian gatehouse in the manner of William Kent. On the right is a Corinthian temple front crumbling and falling to the ground—possibly the one he never executed for Hopetoun.

Adam's sons took over the business and the second Earl kept them on as his architects. John Adam was the eldest, born in 1721; James the youngest; and Robert,

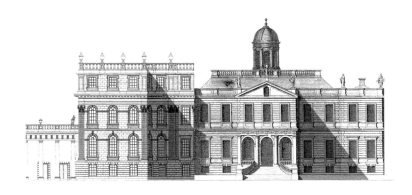

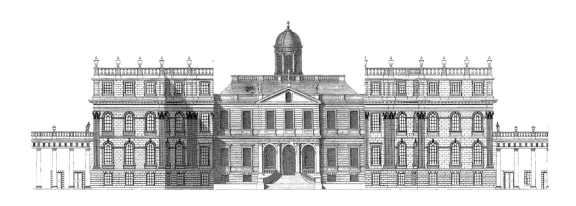

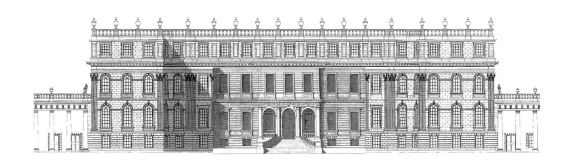

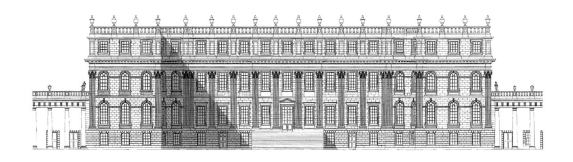

born 1728, proved to be the most brilliant architect by far. At first, work concentrated on completing the much-needed interiors in the southern wing, but also on the immediate surroundings of the house on the east side, including the dyke and ha-ha. In 1750 a decisive step was taken to deal with the unsatisfactory situation in the centre of the main façade. At this stage, the central seven bays of the principal and upper floor were still those of the Bruce house, with a colonnade marking the entrance, banded rustication, windows of smaller size than in the adjoining wings, and possibly the original pediment in front of the mezzanine on top. Several alternative versions of the portico, such a prominent feature of William Adam's design, were tried out on paper before it was decided to abolish it completely. Perhaps tetrastyle temple fronts—chic and desirable when first conceived by William Adam about 1720—had become commonplace by 1750, and monumental pilasters were perceived as the grander alternative, as well as being simpler and more economical. For the detailing *(figs. 75 and 76)*, John Adam went back to the original model, Powis House *(fig. 66)*. Executing this new centrepiece necessitated demolition of both the front wall and some walls behind the façade, as well as rebuilding them with greater thickness and strength. This was carried out very quickly and finished in the summer of 1751.

The new centre is in harmony with the grand and original straight stairway that came next: it is far more monumental and classical than the more conventionally Palladian curved stairs William Adam had planned. As Alistair Rowan has pointed out,[9] the stair is also a technical masterpiece. He praises its functional elegance, seen in the first 'wedge step', designed to be level with the centre of the carriageway paving which falls six inches at the outer edges. Adam also cut two steps out of one block of masonry, thus increasing the mass of the individual stone and at the same time halving the number of horizontal joints. In the stonework and its execution, John Adam proved a worthy successor to his father whose façade, whilst designed to impress the approaching visitor from afar, stands up to close inspection with its sculptural details of astounding quality.

Whilst there is a flavour of French and even Italian Baroque about the east front of Hopetoun, the vocabulary of the architecture is essentially Vitruvian, and this informs all the decorative detail with its classical iconography, no doubt based on illustrated works such as Desgodetz's *Edifices antiques de Rome*. According to the rules of *convenance*, a house like Hopetoun, as the residence of a great nobleman, was entitled to use the full range of elements of dignity, such as monumental Corinthian pilasters and the straight stair leading up to a

◀ *fig. 71a–d*
The stages of construction of Hopetoun's east front, between 1721 and 1751

▼ *fig. 72*
Elevation of the southeast pavilion, originally intended to house the library

Elevation towards the East of the Library *Pavilion at* HOPTOUN

fig. 73
The pediment of
the northeast or
stable pavilion

façade which, even without a pediment and columns, evokes the front of a temple. The urns on the balustrade are a pious reference to the ancestors, the founders of the family and its fortunes; the masks of satyrs evoke Arcadia *(fig. 77a–d)*. As mentioned earlier, the two female figures on either side of the façade at the height of the principal floor represent the family, each sporting an anchor—the anchor being the symbol of *spes* (hope). The figures also hold a cracked globe, referring to the family crest and motto, *at spes non fracta*—'but hope is not broken' *(fig. 78)*.

For any eighteenth-century visitor, identifying the family name with the Christian virtue of *spes* inevitably evoked the other two virtues, *fides* (faith) and particularly *caritas* (love). Love in all its varieties and connotations is always a dominant topic in the imagery of the time, and it is referenced at many points in the interior decoration on which—with the exterior completed thirty years after its inception—attention again focussed from 1750 onwards. The idea of a larger Private Dining Room in the southeast corner of

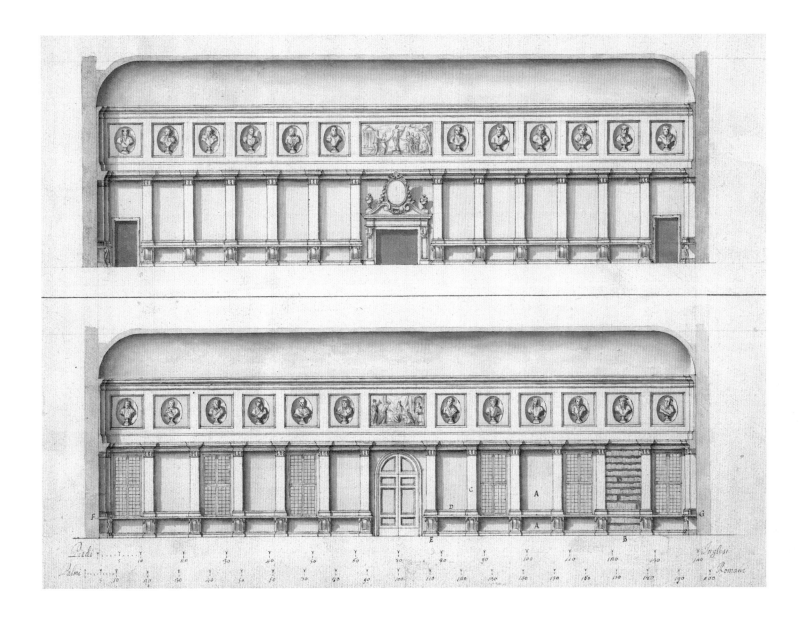

the old Bruce house—part of the *Vitruvius Scoticus* plans which originated in the 1720s—was brought up again. Its counterpart in the plan, the State Dining Room on the northern side of the Bruce house, had already been enlarged between 1728 and 1731. Alternative designs were worked out in great detail in 1752, including the hanging of pictures, but then laid aside, never to be executed *(fig. 79)*. A memorandum by the architects on this topic concludes that the project would be both expensive and disruptive, but this text is also interesting as it highlights a typical situation in a working country house:

> 'the private dining room ... is certainly too small at present when there happens to be a great crowd in it; ... and the placing of a bye table in the little drawing room is always a present relief when a crowd of company happens to come unforeseen.'[10]

This confirms that catering for gatherings of company, sometimes arriving unannounced, was one of the *raisons d'être* of a great house; and a goal of the rebuilding, extending, and furnishing was to cope with this task.

fig. 74
An Italian design for the interior of the Library

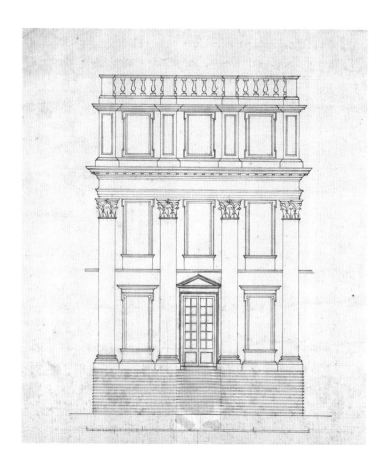

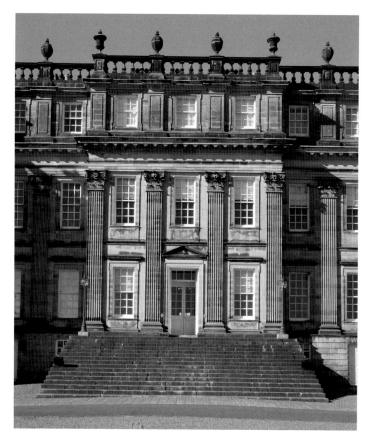

▲ *fig. 75*
Elevation of the
central portion of
the east façade,
presumably drawn
by John Adam

▼ *fig. 76*
The central portion
of the east façade
today

Interiors

With the front completed, the vestibule directly beyond the entrance posed the next problem. Hitherto, the Entrance Hall had been the one designed by William Bruce: a room not unlike the surviving garden parlour beyond the central staircase, both in size and proportion, though somewhat longer. With a fireplace on each side and symmetrically arranged doors it must have been an impressive room, probably not panelled but painted. The demolition and replacement of the façade resulted in a loss of proportion, and the room became far too low for its new incarnation.

There are several alternative designs for the Hall, experimenting with different shapes and decorative schemes, with the grandest arrangement published in *Vitruvius Scoticus*. In the section *(fig. 80)*—which we can compare to the actual situation *(fig. 81)*—it is depicted as a room rising through the full height of both main storeys, with three full-scale upper-floor windows flooding it with light. The separate plate of the Hall *(fig. 82)* roughly tallies with this: elegant Corinthian pilasters and stucco decoration of garlands and cornucopia turn the room into a noble space. A—presumably later—drawing in the archives *(fig. 83)* features less decoration but grander architectural detail, including full columns instead of pilasters. Its reduced height conforms to the space the Hall takes up today, although the actual room is rather restrained and even severe *(fig. 84)*.

The marble for the floor was purchased in Holland, 'a full third cheaper than it would have been at the common British prices', as John Adam proudly stated. The walls are smooth and plain and so is the ceiling; the white friezes and door frames are Vitruvian

▲ *figs. 77a–d*
Satyrs' masks crowning
the east front windows

▼ *fig. 78*
A lead figure of the
allegory of Hope

in character. Classical busts and *tondi*, some of them part of Lord Annandale's Roman purchases, set the tone for a room that is meant to evoke the atrium of an ancient Roman villa. The white marble chimneypiece, with its head of Apollo in a sunburst *(fig. 85)*, was originally, in about 1755, made for the State Bedroom at the northern end of the house, but was transferred to the Hall when the bedroom was replaced by the State Dining Room in 1818. It remains in the spirit of the original concept with its display of pictures of ancestors, portraits of the first and second Marquess of Linlithgow—Governor-General of Australia and Viceroy of India respectively—and of other prominent

fig. 79

Unexecuted design for reordering the Dining Room in the central body of the house, 1725

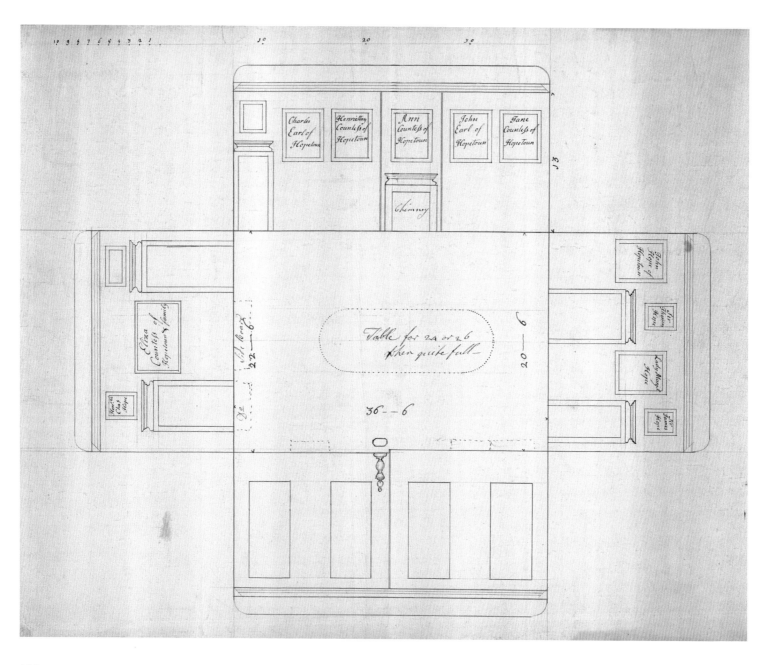

family members, impressing upon visitors that they are entering the house of a family of great tradition and of serious exploits in the ruling of the Empire.

The usual progress through a house of the mid-eighteenth century would have been straight on to a Saloon, but at Hopetoun, the visitors find themselves in the central octagonal staircase of the older house designed by Bruce *(Plates I–III)*. Lord Hopetoun and his architect William Adam must have been in two minds about this. On the one hand, it is an impressive space with beautiful carvings and painted panels, lit by the skylight of the domed tower taken down *circa* 1739; on the other hand, it was already old-fashioned—wooden panelling and carving of this kind were passé. Several designs show how Adam and Hopetoun attempted to tackle the problem. One solution would have been to rip out both the staircase and the ceiling above the Garden Parlour, replacing the latter with a Saloon filling the new, high space. The main floor plan and the section in *Vitruvius Scoticus (figs. 69 and 80)* show what would have been the result of this approach, with a tall space on a square plan replacing the octagonal staircase. Calling it the 'Tribune' indicates an attempt to evoke the domed *Tribuna* in the Uffizi in Florence, a room known to all English *cognoscenti* who visited it on the Grand Tour. The name also has overtones of Courts of Justice, referencing one of the original functions of the Hall in a great house.[11]

There is a separate plate in *Vitruvius Scoticus* showing the four walls of the new double-height Saloon *(fig. 86)*. However, in the section published in the same volume, the Garden Parlour and the room above it are left basically untouched—a contradiction indicating the piecemeal and tentative process of planning. Two beautiful designs for the east and west walls of the Saloon in the archives show this room in greater decorative detail *(fig. 87)*. The topic would have been Mars and Venus, represented by trophies and scallops on the overdoors, fireplace, and oval false windows on the upper level.

But whilst there are significant differences between drawing and engraving, it should be pointed out that both versions of the design would have been impossible to execute; they have, flanking a central fireplace, two entrance doors from the east for which there would simply not have been space on the other side of the wall.

At this stage one begins to wonder just how serious these various designs were meant to be, and if some of them were made partly for the amusement of the Earl and partly for purposes of propaganda and advertisement. In any case, pragmatism prevailed and the central rooms of the Bruce house—the octagonal staircase and the Garden Parlour—were left as they were. Financial considerations will have played an important part, but there were also functional problems that could not be overcome. As *Vitruvius Scoticus* illustrates, Adam was unable to offer a satisfactory solution to the new staircase to the upper floor, and there was no way to connect the Saloon to the suite of new grand rooms.

To enter these, one needs to take a turn from the Hall to the right. What is now the Yellow Drawing Room was originally the Great Dining Room *(Plates XIII–XV and fig. 96)*. Its walls were painted like those of the hall; in the years 1750–4, James Norrie painted both rooms 'four times over' in 'fine white'. Dining rooms were usually painted

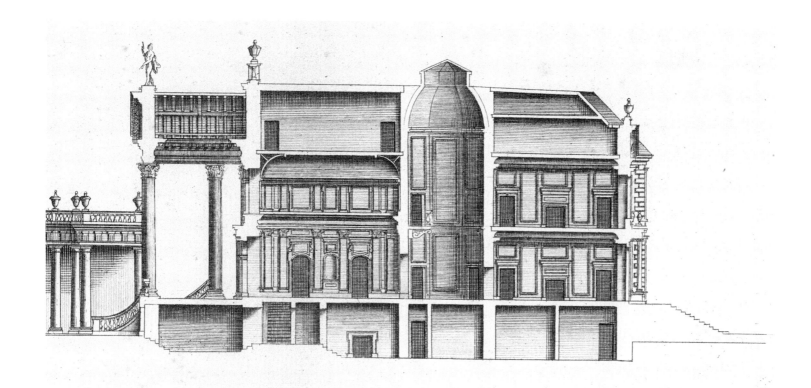

A Section of Hopton House in the midle from East to West

fig. 80

Ideal east–west section through the house featuring a temple front and a two-storey Hall, from *Vitruvius Scoticus*

rather than hung with fabric for fear that textiles would retain food smells. The room's original function can still be seen in the decorative detail of the ceiling and frieze, focusing on Bacchus and his companions in Arcadia, but also referencing Apollo and Diana. Food and wine are represented by grapes and foliage, but the hunt also features prominently, represented by fox and lion masks, bow and arrow-quiver, hunting-club and game-bag. The ceiling cove shows Bacchic youths sporting with elder satyrs, and the topic of love is evoked by Venus's scallop shell.

The Red Drawing Room, next in sequence, is the glory of Hopetoun and by far the most successful of the grand rooms *(Plates XVI and XVII)*. Five great windows looking out to the west give it a scale and rhythm beyond that of any other part of the house. The walls are hung in crimson damask *(fig. 88)*; the stuccoed ceiling is elaborated on the overall topic of 'Peace and Plenty' and is compartmented with a Roman-fashion frame of flowered ribbon-guilloche and the shell badges of Venus. The central medallion is shaped as a *trompe l'œil* dome *(fig. 89)* and its central golden reed-flowered boss was surely intended for a crystal chandelier. Reeds and acanthus foliage spring from cornucopia-scrolled brackets bearing fruit-filled ewers. Brackets between them support exotic birds—such as a parrot and a crane, perched on fruit baskets.

In the ceiling, the Bedchamber end is marked by a curious edifice, a cross between the Vitruvian Primitive Hut (praised by the Abbé Laugier in his *Essai sur l'architecture*, newly published in 1755), a triumphal arch shaped like a Serliana or Venetian window, and a *Chinois* wedding-kiosk *(fig. 90)*. Its frame of marshy reeds is bridged by lozenged and

fig. 81
The actual situation in
a section measured and
drawn in 2011

beribboned cartouches with rustic railings festooned with flowers and Roman acanthus husks. The ends of the ceiling-cove bear harvest cartouches embellished with the baskets of Pomona, goddess of fruitful abundance. Conjoining vines are attributes of the autumnal deity Bacchus, son of Jupiter, and these are clasped by Venus's shells. The banquet of the gods is further recalled by Jupiter's golden eagle displayed by the windows. Symbolising Jupiter's control of the elements, it bears a cartouche displaying the fruit-filled cornucopia of Ceres, deity of agriculture and harvest. A nearby trophy recalls the 'Loves of the Gods' represented by Ovid's history of Cupid and Pan. The Arcadian satyr's love for the water-nymph Syrinx caused the invention of the pipes that bear her name. Pan, confronting the eagle, can be spotted emerging from waved foliage buttressing a bracket that is labelled with a water-scalloped cartouche and dressed by flowers in a wine krater.

Above the projecting hearth, the cove reveals the beribboned and veil-draped golden crown of Pomona. To the left of the chimney-breast, the foliage provides a perch for a watchful crane, and on the right side a parrot, with splayed wings, surveys vines garlanding a lozenged compartment.

For the great fireplace, John Adam originally planned to use a design by William Kent, as published by Isaac Ware, but his rather more creative younger brother Robert, then in Rome, seized the moment to come up with a scheme of his own.[12] The splendid drawing he sent is still in the house *(fig. 91)*. As Adam explains in his accompanying letter dated 3 May 1755, he had 'employed a very Clever fellow to make a Sketch of the Figures & Bas Relievo', using Kent's design as a starting point but bringing it 'as much as possible into the Antique style'. The clever fellow was almost certainly Charles-Louis Clérisseau *(figs. 119 and 120)*, under whose guidance Robert greatly improved his drawing skills during his time in Rome, although other names have also been considered. The sketch was then used as the basis for a contract with the sculptor Michael Rysbrack, whose

fig. 82
South elevation of
the Hall as depicted
in *Vitruvius Scoticus*

fig. 83
A drawing of the
south elevation
of the Hall in an
alternative design

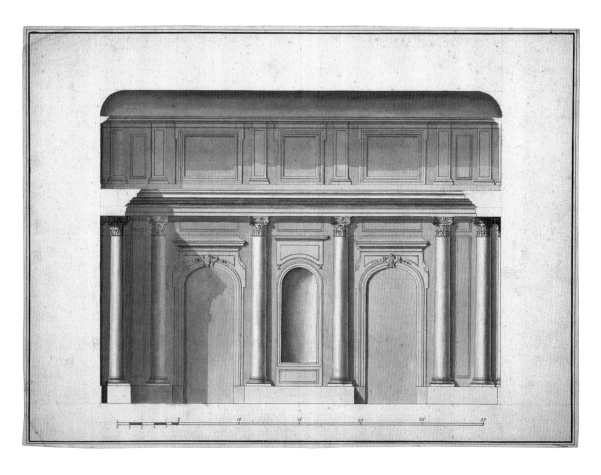

▶ *fig. 85*
Head of Apollo in a
sunburst, tablet of
the Hall fireplace,
originally in the
State Bedroom

▼ *fig. 84*
The Hall as executed

fig. 86
The east elevation of the Saloon, which would have filled the space above the Garden Parlour of the Bruce house. From *Vitruvius Scoticus*

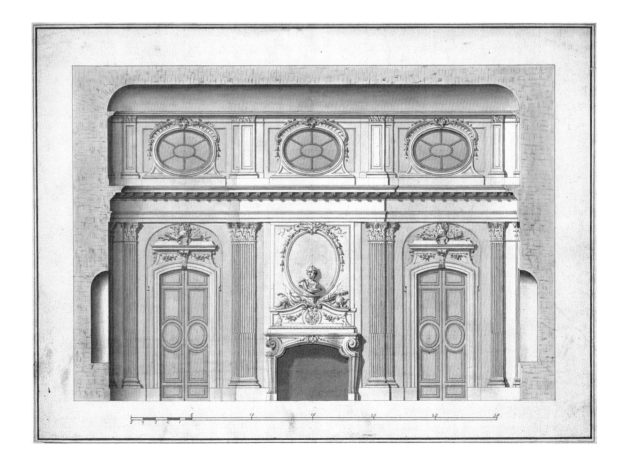

fig. 87
Drawing of an alternative design for the Saloon, reduced in height

signature it bears in acknowledgment of the commission, not as a sign of authorship. Rysbrack was paid the unusually high sum of £600, his contract stipulating that his finished work should be 'on Ship-Board in the Port of London, on or before the first Day of February 1758'.[13]

With its canted pilasters fronted by herms, the chimneypiece design is better viewed sideways *(fig. 92)*, from the entrance to the room, than Kent's conventionally flat and frontal scheme that was favoured originally. The drawing proposed a female figure on the left and a male on the right, probably as alternatives. The choice fell on the female figures which Robert Adam had already recommended as 'propperest' for the Drawing Room, and in the tablet scene *(fig. 93)*, Venus surrounded by playful *amorini* replaced the satyr surprising a nymph, presumably for the same reason. The paired griffins and candelabra were a popular motif at the time, copied from the Temple of Antoninus and Faustina in Rome.

For the pillars between the five west-facing windows, James Cullen provided a design in 1766 for Grecian pier-sconces intended to harmonise with the ceiling and chimneypiece.[14] Mosaic-topped tables of golden alabaster offered surfaces for display. The rooms were, of course, regularly enhanced by elaborate flower arrangements and occasional ornaments *(fig. 94)*, but they really came into their own when filled with ladies and gentlemen in gorgeous dresses and coats, attended by liveried footmen. The mid-eighteenth century was the first and only time when 'it became possible...for a perfectly serious man to attend ceremonies at court in a lavender suit, the waistcoat embroidered with a little silver..., partridge silk stockings, gold buckles, ruffles and lace frill'.[15] But as we have seen, the room's decoration was not merely ornamental. With references to ancient mythology, often cleverly hidden, the ceiling in particular invited visitors to decipher its clues and point them out to each other, as did of course the paintings and their arrangement. Although designed and made by artists and craftsmen, it was understood that the host or patron masterminded the whole scheme, demonstrating his cultivation as well as his political stance through the *Gesamtkunstwerk* of architecture, decoration, and works of art in the house.

The various rooms and their functions were subjected to a number of changes over the following generations. After James Hope succeeded his father as third Earl in 1781, the Dining Room next to the Entrance Hall was converted into a Drawing Room whilst the two rooms adjoining it in the Bruce house were amalgamated as a new Dining Room. This changed yet again

fig. 88
Detail of wall hanging and decor in the Red Drawing Room

following the succession of his half-brother John in 1816. Two years later, under the direction of James Gillespie Graham, the Dining Room was relocated once again, this time to the northernmost of the grand rooms, once the State Bedroom, forming a functional unit with its adjoining Dressing Room, Antechamber, and backstairs *(Plates XIX and XX)*. As we have seen, its chimneypiece survives in the Entrance Hall, and so does the gilt four-poster bed hung with red damask from the workshop of Samuel Norman of London, now in the Bruce Bedchamber *(fig. 114)*. Otherwise we know little of the bedroom's original appearance save for the fact that Robert Adam had a hand in its decoration. Graham merged the bedroom and the dressing room into one larger space in 1818 and gave it a splendid neoclassical appearance, in time for a visit by Leopold of Saxe-Coburg-Saalfeld, widower of Princess Charlotte of Wales and later King of the Belgians. In 1822, George IV dined here on the last day of his visit to Scotland; on his arrival at Hopetoun, the Company of Archers lined the steps *(fig. 11)*.

◄ *fig. 89*
The ceiling of the
Red Drawing Room

🔺 *fig. 90*
Detail of the
northern part of
the ceiling in the
Red Drawing Room

133

fig. 91
Design for the fireplace
in the Red Drawing Room,
drawn probably by
Charles-Louis Clérisseau,
to be executed by the
sculptor Michael Rysbrack

An assessment

As the rooms work extremely well on their own terms, one does not usually try and relate them to the exterior of the house. William Adam's plans, elevations, and sections of the house—published much later in *Vitruvius Scoticus*—seem perfectly logical in themselves. Only on comparison of the engraved drawings with a survey of the actual fabric does it become apparent how cleverly they gloss over architectural contradictions and weaknesses. Starting with the depiction of the Hall in Adam's section of the house *(fig. 80)*, we see that it should have taken up the full height of the two main floors, three windows on the upper level flooding it with light. As the actual section *(fig. 81)* shows, it does not fill the whole space but leaves room for a somewhat cramped half-storey whose floor cuts awkwardly across the great upper-floor windows, with only their top part open. If we look at the north–south section *(fig. 95)*, we find a similarly

fig. 92
The fireplace in the
Red Drawing Room

fig. 93
The tablet and frieze
of the fireplace in
the Red Drawing
Room

fig. 94
Detail of the Red
Drawing Room Fireplace

unsatisfactory spatial arrangement relating to the State Rooms on the northern side. The high coved ceilings of the State Dining Room (now the Yellow Drawing Room) and the Red Drawing Room project upwards into the space that—according to the elevation—should have been filled by rooms of roughly equal grandeur to those on the principal floor. Furthermore, the former State Bedroom (now the Dining Room) is attached to the main house in a less than fluent way.

All this indicates that Adam and Hopetoun understood elevations and plans but were less sure when it came to planning in three dimensions. It should be said that the problem is not apparent in the part of the house that was executed first, the southern addition, as the rooms of this wing, on both main floors, fit very well behind the façade and between the floor levels determined by the Bruce house. But the large formal rooms in the north range, particularly the Dining and the Drawing Room, needed the appropriate soaring height of their coved ceilings, and this was less easily accommodated.

Looking at a great house that has evolved over time, it is always fascinating to speculate about the reasoning behind the various stages of its development: what made patron and architect espouse a specific approach? What problems did they have to cope with? What were their aims and priorities? When William Bruce was first charged with designing and building a house on the site, he found himself in an ideal situation. He had virgin ground to build on, no existing fabric, and plenty of space to site the structure. His patrons were keen, enthusiastic, and they had plenty of money. Furthermore, Bruce had an experienced workforce to hand. All this made it quite easy to build and complete the new house fairly quickly.

The situation in which Lord Hopetoun and William Adam found themselves in the 1720s was quite different. There was an existing building that had cost a substantial amount of money. It was still fairly new and in good condition, and we may assume that the family were fond of it, given that it was comfortable enough, if a little small and outdated. Simply pulling it down and starting over on a greater scale was not an option. Money was always an issue in the building and furnishing of a great house, and means and ambitions were not always on a par. Lord Hopetoun was comfortably off rather than obscenely rich. He did not have the cash to see his great new house built in one fell swoop. But as others had found, it was quite possible to build a large and splendid house out of the annual income from the estate and from various lucrative offices. It must be remembered just how long such schemes could take: at Hopetoun, rebuilding started in 1721 and was not properly completed until the end of the 1760s. The duration of the building process may be indicative less of the tardiness of the workforce than of the availability of funds per annum.

Aware of the prospect that building would be going on for many years, patron and architect did not feel the need to produce a detailed and consistent set of plans for the

fig. 95
North–south section through Hopetoun House, looking east. The section features on the main floor (from right to left): part of the Hall, the Yellow Drawing Room, the Red Drawing Room, and the State Bedroom; and it illustrates certain discrepancies between the east façade and the interiors behind it

whole building before starting with the wing that was needed most urgently. From then on, it was a gradual transformation, step by step, working towards the final goal, with detailed plans made as and when they were actually needed. There was no sweeping demolition, no making space for a grand new scheme: on the contrary, one of the most striking characteristics of the transformation process is that nothing was wasted. Economy can be seen in many decisions and actions over the years—doing without things that might have been desirable, like the large Private Dining Room that had been planned so painstakingly, meant that in the end money could be spent where it produced the greatest effect, such as on the State Rooms.

As we have seen, the approach meant that much of the grand new front had little to do with the interior structure behind it, and there were unsatisfactory rooms in the upper reaches of the house above the Hall and the Grand Apartment. We cannot know how the first Earl and William Adam felt about these well-concealed inadequacies; perhaps they cheerfully accepted the awkward spaces hidden behind the façade as an inevitable consequence of the patron's priorities and constraints. But William Adam deserves praise for the quality of the stone masons' work which informs the whole house, and he certainly did a wonderful job in producing a 'propaganda' version of the house for his posthumously published work, *Vitruvius Scoticus*, glossing over Hopetoun's contradictions and showing it as it might have been.

One person who knew the real structure of the house extremely well and who was aware of its inadequacies was Robert Adam. A gifted and ambitious young architect, Robert must have fretted over the many incongruities hidden behind Hopetoun's façade. How else should one interpret his seemingly light-hearted and facetious suggestion to Lord Hopetoun in 1755, that he should 'pull down his whole House that I may have the satisfaction to try my Genious on a new one'?[16]

XVI / XVII The Red
Drawing Room

XVIII–XX   Impressions of the
State Dining Room and
view along the enfilade

Dining Room.

		Feet. Inch.	Feet.
Plaister Walls	Ft. In. 11.6		3392
2 Coats	by 83.4	958 4	
Deduce for Pictures and Chimney Glasses ✓ Note		394 8	563
North Side.			
Picture Frames		8 —	
	5 times by	— 4	13
More Do.		8 —	
	2 times by	— 6	8
More Do.		12 6	
	by	— 6	6
More Do.		20 10	
	2 times by	— 7	24
West Side.			
Picture Frames		16 6	
	2 times by	— 6	16
More Do.		12 8	
	2 times by	— 6	12
More Do.		16 9	
South Side.	by	1 2	19
Picture Frames		6 3	

chapter 6

Dining Room. continued

			Feet. Inch.		Feet. Inch.	
South Side – continued.					4066	10
Picture Frames						
	2 times by		–	6	13	–
More D?			30	–		
	by		–	8	20	–
More D?			12	8		
	by		–	6	6	4
Glass Frames			9	–		
one Coat, all carved.	2 times by		4	1	73	6
Surbase Lining			76	–		
one Coat	by		3	6	266	–
Doors, Architrave, Cornice & Tympany			13	2		
one Coat all carved.	4 times by		6	4	333	6
Back of 2 Doors in Wester Passage			8	6		
3 Coat	2 times by		4	2	70	10
Scuncheons & Sophets of D?			21	–		
1 Coat.	by		3	3	68	3
Presses in D? Passage			7	5		
3 Coats	2 times by		8	6	126	1
Shelfs of D?			2	9		

Colour Schemes in the Yellow Drawing Room

by Alexandra Skedzuhn-Safir

The visual appearance of historic rooms, as defined by surface colours or fabrics, is often taken for granted by today's visitors: rarely are they aware that what they see is only the latest layer in a long sequence of paint schemes, some of which may have been markedly different from the present one. Or they may even be looking at a fairly recent academic recreation of one of the former schemes (often with an element of guesswork involved), or simply a colour scheme reflecting today's taste in architectural colour.

Surfaces decay and are subjected to daily wear and tear. Thus they require regular renewal, and, obviously, rooms and spaces have always been adapted to the changing tastes of successive generations. Sometimes the function and use of a room changes, requiring dramatic reinterpretation and different colours and materials.

The possibilities of paint research

But is it possible to reveal how things appeared in the past? Can we ever determine what an entire room looked like at a specific period?

Investigation of the architectural surface as well as other primary sources, such as historical accounts, photographs, prints, memoranda, or travelogues, can shed light on the appearance of a room at a specific stage. Ideally, paint layers can be related to time periods and to those who commissioned a specific decorative scheme for an individual room or for an entire house.

However, paint research can also serve to establish who the artists and craftsmen were, which structural changes were made within the building, and the period in which the surfaces were painted.[1] Paint examination is of vital relevance for art historians, architectural historians, and conservators. Ideally, investigations are carried out in collaboration with other disciplines. Examining technological aspects serves to document material findings and reflects changes or development in technology. Additionally, it supports research into the causes of damage, as well as previous conservation or restoration interventions.[2]

Overleaf
Detail from the accounts in the archives

There are several ways of investigating painted architectural surfaces, and new methods are being developed all the time. Which method is employed depends primarily on the research question, but also on the painting technique, materials, and the surface onto which the paint was applied.

Generally speaking, both non-invasive and invasive methods can be used. Non-invasive methods do not damage or alter the chemical or physical properties of the analysed material. Significant information can be obtained by scrutinising surfaces, and a simple, effective method is to look at a surface texture with a raking light, which can reveal not only structural damage but also underlying surface decoration imperceptible in daylight alone.

Invasive investigation methods are those that produce a visible or even non-visible alteration or destruction of the painted architectural surface—uncovering successive paint layers, for example, or taking samples of paint.

On-site investigation in which paint layers are carefully removed can reveal the stratigraphy of coatings on any given surface, be it wood, stucco, or plaster. Depending on the situation, paint layers can be taken off mechanically or with the use of solvents. Ideally, each different architectural feature is sampled, sometimes in different areas, to ensure that findings are representative and consistent throughout the interior. This method can help to establish not just colour but also decorative finishes such as graining and marbling, or stencilled and painted patterns and images.

Dating and concordance

To determine how the various paint layers of architectural features are interrelated, a variety of methods can be employed. One is to uncover the layers from two adjoining features; another is to establish a concordance of all uncovered paint layers and to relate the various findings. The concordance is basically a method of relating the layers from every sample area and recording these in a table.

The techniques developed in below-ground archaeology have yielded a number of different dating methods which can also be employed in such investigations.[3] Sometimes

fig. 96
The Yellow Drawing
Room and its ceiling

it is possible to establish an absolute date for a paint layer, at other times only relative dates can be ascertained, as in *terminus ante quem* or *terminus post quem*.[4]

In practice, however, these two methods—cross-sectioning and uncovering of paint layers—do not necessarily provide enough evidence to establish a relative or absolute date. This could be because neighbouring architectural features are not directly physically 'connected', or because two or more non-connected architectural features have differing layers of paint. So any statement on how a specific paint layer of one feature correlates to another must remain, in a sense, purely speculative. Also, it may be the case that paint layers of architectural elements were removed, especially those that were damaged or had been painted so many times that the detail in delicate carvings had become obscured.

The Yellow Drawing Room

As an example of how the colour scheme of a room has changed over the decades, our investigation at Hopetoun was focused on one room in particular: the Yellow Drawing Room *(Plates XIII–XV and fig. 96)*. Initially, this was the State Dining Room. The research focussed on the on-site removal of successive paint layers, optical analysis of cross-section paint samples, and the documentary evidence of the Hopetoun House archive. The paint examination was documented with photographs, concordance lists, and international colour codes. The colours uncovered with the removal of the different paint layers were reproduced in aquarelle.

Today, the panelling, windows, shutters, doors, and cornice are painted in an off-white cream colour, and the ceiling in a very soft rose hue—hardly noticeable in the delicate electric light. The windows on the east wall have wooden shutters that are folded back into recesses when not in use. The panelling covers three sides of the room, with part-gilt carved mouldings.

The dominant feature of the walls on the south, west, and north sides is the yellow silk damask wall hanging—a Napoleonic fern-and-wreath design[5] framed by a gilt wooden fillet. The transition from wall to ceiling is marked by a cavetto moulding, and the walls are separated by a part-gilt cornice; the ceiling itself is richly decorated in stucco. But what lies beneath these coloured surfaces and textures?

A reconstruction

Analysis of relevant accounts of the room across the decades reveals a great deal about the changing schemes. As early as 1742, an account by the painter James Norrie mentions the Dining Room as having been painted in a white oil paint, along with elements in colours other than white, also in oil paint.[6] This may point to the white plastered walls, appropriate for a dining room, with a grey employed for the architectural features, namely the mouldings and three friezes which Norrie then 'enriched' in 1742/3, as they were considered to be too light. In fact, Robert Adam commented in 1755 that the dining room walls were painted white.[7]

The next changes to this room were made between 1752 and 1758 when the joiner John Patterson made the wooden doors and window frames.[8]

In a 1768 account, the painter Duglas McLaurin charged for painting the plaster walls with two coats and for applying one coat to the carved elements, as well as to the doors, architrave, cornice, and tympana *(fig. 97)*.[9]

fig. 97
Detail from the accounts from 1768 regarding the painting of architectural features in several rooms

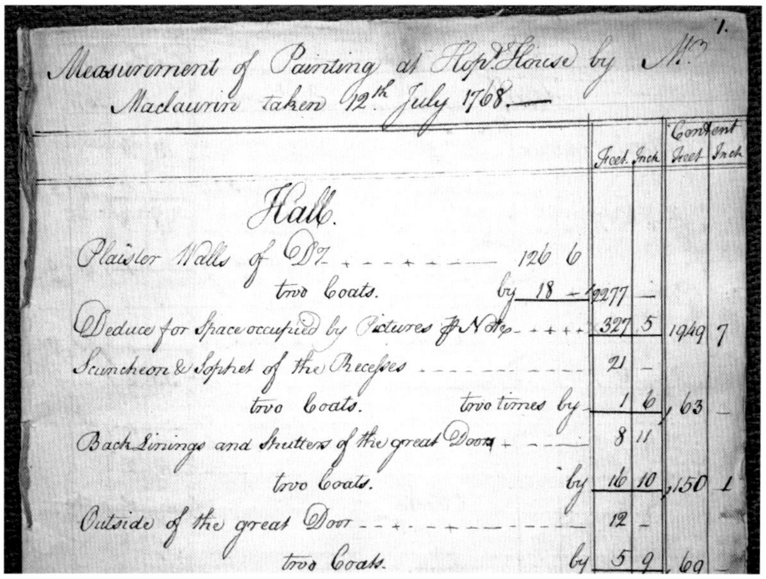

151

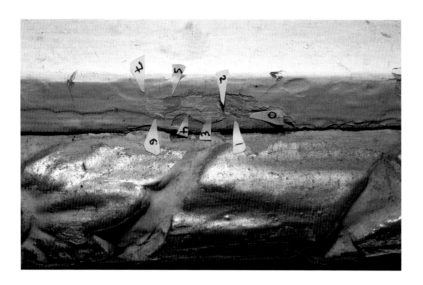

▲ *fig. 98*
Area 1 in this detail may
well show the grey paint
applied by McLaurin in 1768

▼ *fig. 99*
Detail of one of John
Dawson's rococo
cartouches from the 1750s

Note of expense of Painting & Gilding of Drawing Room, Hopetoun House, as taken from Mr Bonar's Acct 1819. —

Painting — x — £98 — £58.7.10½
Gilding — 159.19.7
£218.7.5½

To this should be added £40 — the ceiling being done at 6d & 2d — that of the Saloon (in Gilt) is 1/6.

Expence of Saloon in 1827.

Painting — £76.2.2
Gilding — 136.3.6
£212.5.8

N.B. The acct of 1827 includes the expence of Gilding Tables & Mirror Frames — in all £47.2.6. —

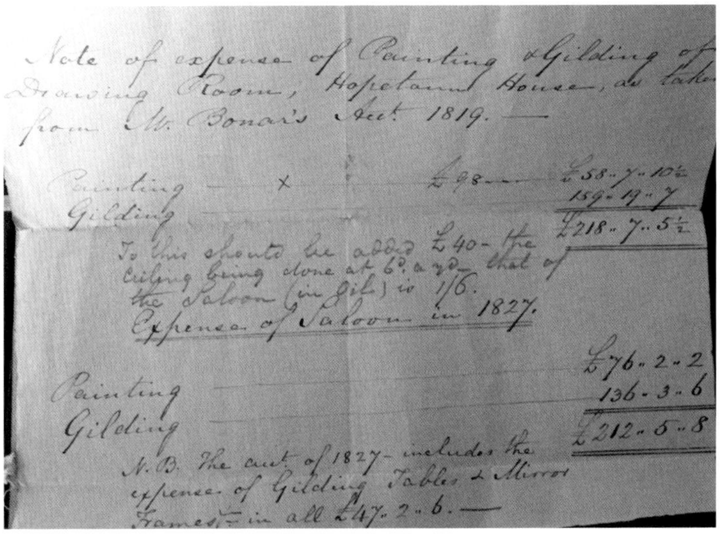

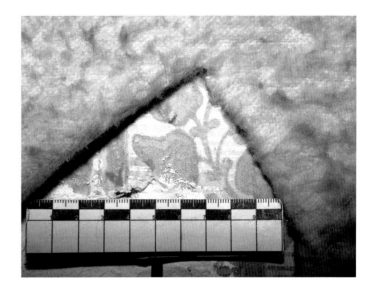

It may well be that the paintwork carried out in 1768 by McLaurin represents the first layer in greyish beige on the panelling, doorframes, and windows *(fig. 98)*.[10] So far, the plaster walls had been painted twice: in 1742 and, most likely, between 1752 and 1758, when the other works were carried out. This is supported by findings which have revealed two very distinct and easily separable layers of paint, indicative of the time lapse between them.

According to the account by McLaurin, the 'roofs' (presumably the ceiling) were 'whitened'. In fact, this layer of unbound chalk can easily be washed off or 'turned', and could not be detected during the paint research.[11] In the 1750s, the Yellow Drawing Room had been fitted in rococo style with a lavish stuccoed ceiling design created by the plasterer John Dawson *(figs. 96 and 99)*.[12] Quite possibly the ceiling was painted soon afterwards, as evinced by the many paint layers. Today, the oldest paint layer is a grey colour, followed by a greenish beige, painted at some point after 1768.

The overall effect of a mainly white or very light-coloured room is in line with neo-Palladian tastes, when white, off-white, or shades of white (referred to as 'stone colour' and 'pearl colour') were considered to be less sensitive to light. And the cost of lighting a room would be relatively low, as fewer candles would have been needed.[13]

The next record of expenses was for the decoration by a Mr Bonar of this room, referred to as the Drawing Room *(fig. 100)*.[14] This account lists the painting and gilding work carried out in 1819. The rather austere and low-key decorative scheme of the second half of the eighteenth century was replaced sometime after the 1760s.[15] Playfulness and *joie de vivre* are now reflected in the flocked wallpaper, light pink background, floral motifs, and horizontal hand-painted thin lines of gold powder *(fig. 101)*.[16] The black bole underneath the gold leaf was fashionable in Great Britain for gildings in the latter half of the eighteenth century.[17] Therefore it is probable that the gilt wooden fillet hiding the tacks of the wall hanging was made especially for the flocked wallpaper, and both gold colours harmonise perfectly.

On-site research has revealed a painting technique known as 'picking in'. This was employed on painted stucco ornaments such as flowers and fruit to render them more vivid and three-dimensional. This meant that the complete ceiling was painted in a lighter red-orange colour, and subsequently the ornaments were covered in a darker red

▼ ***fig. 100***
Record of the painting and gilding carried out in 1827 in the Yellow Drawing Room

▲ ***fig. 101***
The rose-coloured wallpaper with flocked floral pattern and thin horizontal lines in gold powder covered the walls of the Yellow Dining Room after the 1760s. The original colour may well have been a more vivid rose or even red

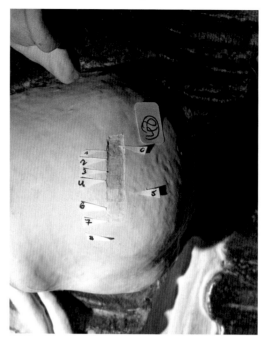

figs. 102a+b
Overview and detail of the area examined. The fruit has a number of paint layers: basis (0), bluish grey (1), light grey (2), light orange (3), rose-red (4), light yellow (5), warm rose (6), white (7), visible paint layer (8)

tone *(figs. 102a+b)*. This is a stylistic element often found in the neo-classical period.[18] The evidence is not clear as to whether some decorative elements of the ceiling were already gilded when the ornaments were picked in, though it seems likely that the background was painted in a shade of grey. It would have been unusual, however, and not in vogue at the time, to have used different gold tones for architectural elements in one room.[19]

However, according to the 1819 account by Mr Bonar, he gilded the mouldings, architrave, and cornice in the 'Drawing Room'.[20] Whether or not this relates to decorative elements that today have two separate layers of gold *(fig. 103)*—such as the doors (including pediments and door frames), the panelling, and the windows—cannot be known for sure, as these areas are subjected to daily wear and tear and concomitant repainting. This makes it extremely difficult to determine which paint layers belong together chronologically and which paint layers may be missing.

Hidden secrets of the accounts

Many of the accounts mention the use of white lead, as well as red lead, vermillion red, umber, and verdigris.[21] Often the descriptions of colours, rather than pigments, are listed, such as iron colour, pearl colour, stone colour, or wainscot colour.[22] These were known as 'common colours'. Linguistically, accounts also reveal how everyday objects had an effect on measurements of liquids or volumes. 'Mutchkin' (from the term *mutch*, a kind of cap) and 'chopin' (from the French liquid measure *chopine*), for example, are Scottish units of measurement for volumes, the first one equalling 212 ml, the latter 848 ml. Both measures went out of use towards the end of the nineteenth century when imperial measures were introduced.

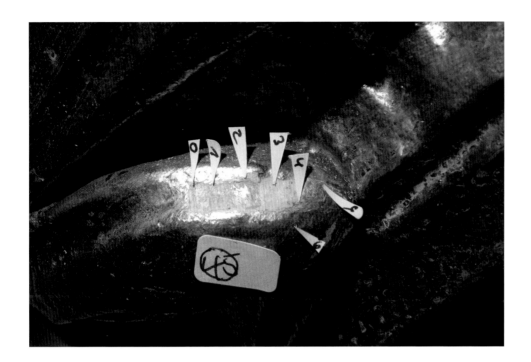

fig. 103
In some gilded architectural
elements, as in this sample
from the ceiling, two layers
of gold leaf can be detected

History unravelled

The records of the Hopetoun House archive that are relevant to this architectural paint investigation date for the most part from the eighteenth century. Quite possibly many more records once existed, but have been lost.

At moments, these accounts remain unclear as to what exactly they refer to; but this is not as unusual as it may appear, considering that, at the time the accounts were written, it was easily understood between the parties what was being referred to and which kind of work was being carried out. Such knowledge, however, is not the only evidence that is now inaccessible, but the washed off or removed paint layers will also remain forever lost to us. Thus, the reconstruction of the architectural colour schemes may be well informed, but must nevertheless remain conjecture.

When relating documentary evidence with physical evidence, it is absolutely vital to keep an open mind to alternative interpretations, even if they seem to contradict former conclusions. Research work also shows that, even when there is no hard evidence to prove something, that is not proof that such a thing did not occur. Therefore, one should not present a finding without leaving room for potential alternatives. And some 'truths' may indeed never be revealed.

The layering of coats of paint, and determining whether former colour schemes were adopted or radically rejected, provides a rich testimony to the fashions and changing requirements that successive generations brought to these rooms.

chapter 7

Furniture at Hopetoun

by David Jones

Hopetoun is Scotland's key 'improvement' house of the early eighteenth century, in the fields of both architecture and furniture. Sir William Bruce had created the most original and contemporary French-style parade house for the first Earl at the turn of the seventeenth century, and this was enlarged by William, John, and Robert Adam between 1723 and 1756 to become, in the mid-eighteenth century, the model to which other builders and furnishers aspired.

Although the Bruce interiors of 1699–1703 were comfortably wood-panelled in the Scots-Dutch manner, there is some evidence that the furniture was progressively French in style. Corner and side tables remain from this date, including a water-gilt example *(fig. 104)* in the style of Jean Pelletier against the south wall of the Garden Room or 'Saloon' which compares favourably with tables by the same master cabinet maker at Windsor Castle. Pelletier's son-in-law, the Huguenot carver and cabinet maker John Guilbaud, also employed by the royal family in London, supplied a chimney glass and three pairs of wall sconces to Hopetoun in 1703. Luxury trades were being encouraged in Edinburgh and French craftsmen were being courted to set up business there, provided they recruited local apprentices. Jacques and Henri Hieu (Hue) and Daniel Le Gagett were Parisian masters licenced to operate in the capital just as Hopetoun was setting a trend for French glamour in the domestic arts.

In due course, the French Baroque wall furniture was replaced with new architectural designs inspired by Palladio, mainly the work of William Strachan, a carver and gilder of Aberdonian descent. Strachan was busy in the 1740s providing modern decoration both for old tower houses such as Dundas Castle and for striking new Palladian compositions such as House of Dun, one of William Adam's northern commissions. He was known for his gilt architectural chimney glasses, of which several examples survive, but the best of his work is in what is now the Writing Closet (originally a dressing room) at Hopetoun *(fig. 105)*. This, with stepped, scrolled and shouldered stiles beneath a broken pediment, was supplied in 1742 to surmount an existing corner fireplace. He also made picture frames for the family portraits now displayed in the State Dining Room. Strachan is important for Hopetoun because he came to work for the second Earl having completed the interior woodwork at Newhailes, that miniature but perfect

Overleaf
Detail of a side
table in the Hall

fig. 104
Water-gilt side
table in the
Garden Room

Enlightenment house just outside Musselburgh whose new interiors were commissioned by Sir James Dalrymple after 1721. Newhailes can be seen as a testing ground for talented Scottish craftsmen who progressed to larger scale works at Hopetoun. Thomas Clayton the plasterer, William Strachan the carver and gilder, and, later, Thomas Welsh the cabinet maker, all came directly from Newhailes to Hopetoun.

There is a letter in the Hopetoun archive from Sir James Dalrymple of 23 October 1750, recommending Thomas Welsh. In addition to discussing mining matters, the two lairds were sharing information about the best wrights working around Edinburgh—men who could be encouraged and trained up. In a small country such as Scotland, this was a typical pattern; the leading landowners knew one another and were active in patronising the same good tradesmen who were 'passed on' from house to house. Thomas Welsh was officially engaged at Hopetoun shortly after the recommendation from

fig. 105
Chimney glass in
the Writing Closet

Dalrymple, and he subsequently enjoyed a thirty-year career on the estate, becoming a salaried employee who was allowed to take on apprentices. He was privileged to own a copy of Thomas Chippendale's *Director;* this unique first edition survives accompanied by its original receipt whilst the Earl's own subscription copy was sold at Sotheby's in 1889. The proliferation of *Director* copies underlines the importance in Scotland of this furniture pattern book, but it was an expensive publication, usually beyond the means of the ordinary wright. The Earl of Hopetoun seems to have treated his employee well—he was generously paid (two shillings a day according to his 1758 contract) and was most probably helped to buy his own copy of the *Director,* supplied at a special discount by the Edinburgh bookseller Gavin Hamilton.

Welsh made most of the seat furniture at Hopetoun, including the 'parade' chairs and sofas for the State Drawing Room. He emulated Chippendale's French chair designs, but added trademark high-knuckled ball and claw feet which do not appear in the *Director.* Many of his chairs have carved shell knees that replicate carved woodwork details found at Newhailes, but the characteristic feet and other elements such as arm terminals are taken from a remarkable pattern chair *(fig. 106)* that was supplied in 1758 by the Edinburgh Upholstery Company—a cooperative partnership with a stock of fashionable furniture sold from Carrubber's Close between 1754 and 1759. Scottish tradesmen James Cullen and Alexander Peter were principal players in this enterprise but supplied furniture to Hopetoun in their own right during the 1750s and 1760s. The second Earl gave the fledgling Edinburgh Upholstery Company a great deal of business, as reflected in the six-page discharge delivered in 1759, bound in a pretty lattice pattern wallpaper cover that survives in the archive *(fig. 107).*

As well as hanging paper throughout the house, the company supplied carpets and various items of furniture, mainly carved, including looking glass and marble slab table frames. Lord Hopetoun's patronage was of key importance, and the Edinburgh Upholstery Company is another example of local craftsmen who benefited from his encouragement. Around the house there is a supporting cast of anonymous brown

fig. 106
Pattern chair by the
Edinburgh Upholstery
Company

furniture that is nevertheless distinctively Scottish and was fashionable for its time. Examples are shown in *figures 108 and 109*; a chair with paper-roll cresting and a 'bed-room table' with a single long flap hanging down the back.

No new house of any pretension in Scotland was without items by Alexander Peter, and Hopetoun had its complement. But this was not furniture for the main public rooms as at Dumfries and Haddo where Peter provided showpieces with carved ornament. For Hopetoun, between 1757 and 1758, he executed practical pieces such as presses and wainscot desks. However, the Earl probably set an important example in employing him, and Peter appears in subsequent commissions that involved his recommendation. For instance, Lord Hopetoun took a central role in the design stage of Dumfries House on the west coast of Scotland. He had employed John and Robert Adam at Hopetoun,

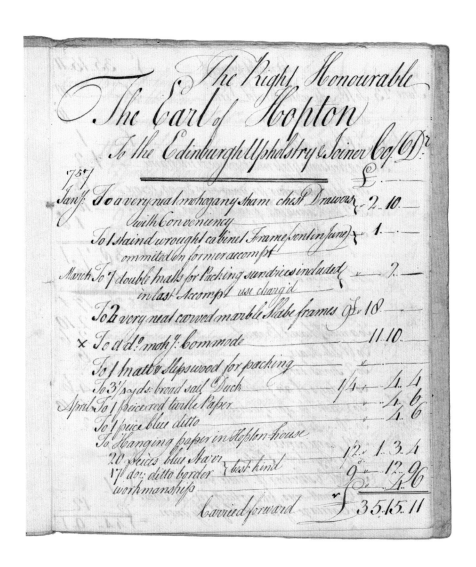

fig. 107
First page of a bill
from the Edinburgh
Upholstery Company
for work between 1757
and 1759

whom he recommended to Lord Dumfries, and it cannot be entirely coincidental that Alexander Peter went on to make over 200 pieces for this new Palladian mansion in Ayrshire upon its completion in 1757.

It is certainly evident that the second Earl made things happen, gathering in the best local expertise for the execution of his pieces, but he was not a professional house decorator. For the 'look' of Hopetoun, he depended upon the services of an extraordinary impresario of the cabinet making trade—James Cullen—who coordinated the furnishing of his house between 1753 and 1773. Cullen was an expatriate Roman-Catholic Scot living in Soho, London, who had worked for the successful Lancashire-born cabinet maker and upholsterer William Bradshaw at his premises in Greek Street. Bradshaw himself had been cabinet maker to the Dukes of Atholl and Hamilton, and so represented that small group of exclusive tradesmen who were patronised by the Scots gentry when in London. Significantly, Cullen was involved in the management of London clubs, notably the Ladies' Club, or Coterie, of Arlington Street, which numbered five dukes amongst its membership. It was probably this social *milieu* that helped Cullen in his career as house furnisher and interior decorating consultant; it is therefore no surprise that in the second Earl's mid-eighteenth century improvements are found several similarities to English ducal country house interiors. A little insight into Cullen's work schedule is given by a letter of 22 July 1766 in which he informs Lord Hopetoun: 'I have a large house to furnish in Northamptonshire where I must go soon—then Ld Abercorn at Duddiston [*sic*] in summer.' He must have been one of the most well-travelled decorators in the country.

According to plan, the important furniture at Hopetoun was displayed along one major axis, or *enfilade*, which was the longest example in Scotland at the time, occupying a row of nine rooms across the central range of the house. This arrangement was itself rather English because hitherto the State Apartments in Scottish houses had been spirally, not horizontally, aligned. Melville, Newhailes, and Mavisbank are examples. The new axial design required the furniture to be lined up as if for military inspection, in a straight sequence that became richer and finer as it progressed from Saloon to State Bedroom. So for the Hall, Cullen specified a relatively restrained scheme involving twelve hall chairs and two 'large hall benches', echoing the couches found in the entrance vestibules of Roman villas. These benches, originally painted white, could be

▼ *fig. 108*
Chair by the Edinburgh
Upholstery Company

▲ *fig. 109*
Bedroom table
by the Edinburgh
Upholstery
Company

carried outside in fair weather, a Scots tradition of indoor-outdoor seating that is recorded in several eighteenth-century houses along the east coast, including Durie and Raith, Fife; Arniston and Newhailes, Midlothian; and Paxton, Berwickshire.

Immediately to the right of the entrance to the Dining Room was a pair of gilt pier glasses and tables awaiting inspection. These, like the hall benches, were the work of the Edinburgh Upholstery Company, but in a more elaborately decorative style, enriched with upward-thrusting fronds characteristic of Scottish rococo work. (To economise, one of the carved frames was glazed with old glass already in the Earl's possession, resulting in a discount of £8.)

Continuing the promenade into the Red Drawing Room or Grand Apartment, the visitor's attention is drawn to the left, where a much grander spectacle of four carved glasses and console tables occupies the window piers of the west wall *(figs. 110 and 111)*. An immediate similarity can be seen between these wall furnishings and those in the saloon at Holkham, Norfolk, where four glasses and tables attributed to James Whittle and Samuel Norman take the same position against crimson silk damask. This partnership specialising in the creation of looking glasses had supplied similar models to Petworth and Woburn Abbey—both palatial houses with furniture collections of ducal quality. There was little economy in the Red Drawing Room at Hopetoun, as Cullen had

fig. 110
Console tables and
glasses in the Red
Drawing Room

specified wide, oval glasses similar to those at Woburn and Holkham, of greater expense and higher status than other shapes. A 20 per cent glass tax had been reintroduced in 1745, making the material very costly, and these mirrors display an impressive width of the expensive material. The frames were designed to fit right to the edges of the wall piers, and the curtains were made especially narrow to enhance the effect. The pendant oval form of the glasses was the height of fashion when they were installed in the summer of 1768 but it was inevitable that, in the ten years or so it had taken to create this furnishing sequence, style preferences would have changed. The marble slabs for the console tables had been ordered from Italy by Robert Adam in 1755 and their carved supports were in place by 1766. By the time it came to ordering the pier glasses, almost certainly supplied by the pre-eminent London makers Whittle and Norman, the vogue was for ovals with flat, moulded frames that hung from gilded ribbands and scrolls. Thus, the Hopetoun pier ensemble began as a rococo composition but was finished in a style that anticipated the coming neoclassicism of the later eighteenth century.

Thomas Welsh, the talented estate wright, made two sofas, six chairs, and eight elbow chairs for the room 'finish'd and put in their places' on 16 January 1768, exactly as Cullen had recommended in his original memo to the second Earl, dated July 1758 *(figs. 112 and 113)*. These were upholstered in the same crimson silk 'brought from abroad by a nobleman' that Cullen had acquired for the walls of the apartment. In a fascinating correspondence between the decorator and the Earl, dated 1767, gilt borders for the silk hangings are discussed and it was concluded that cast lead would be considerably cheaper than *papier mâché*, as was first suggested. This is of interest as the Hopetoun family fortune had originated from lead mining.

If the furnishing of the State Apartment at Hopetoun began quietly with white-painted lobby furniture by the Edinburgh Upholstery Company, it reached a grand climax in the Bedroom and Dressing Room. Here, in gilded and domed finery, was one of the great State Beds of Scotland *(fig. 114)*. Taking Thomas Chippendale's definition of this type as a benchmark, the Hopetoun Bed is a hybrid of 'Best' and 'State' models. In Scottish terms (and it must be remembered that such things were objects of intense

competition) it can be compared with the new state bed made by William Masters for the Duke of Atholl in 1756, and Chippendale's own 'Best' bed made for the Earl of Dumfries in 1759. But the Hopetoun Bed of 1768 is more elaborate that either of these. It makes lavish use of crimson silk damask. With double valance and other generous detailing, it uses much more than the 150 yards of crimson Genoa damask specified for the bed at Blair, and it has a greater quantity of damask-covered carving than the Dumfries House bed. The fact that the tester and cornice are gilded and domed makes this a bed of considerable height and impact. In English terms it is comparable with the great state bed at Petworth, commissioned by the second Earl of Egremont. 'Mr Norman' is noted as the supplier of the Hopetoun Bed in a letter of 1768 from Cullen to the Earl, the decorator stating that 'we have finally concluded the bargain last week.' In

fig. 111
Console table in the
Red Drawing Room

165

▲ *fig. 112*
Sofa in the Red
Drawing Room

➤ *fig. 114*
The Hopetoun Bed

◄ *fig. 113*
Elbow chair in the
Red Drawing Room

fig. 115
One of two bombé
commodes in the Yellow
Drawing Room

view of the fact that this was written on 2 February 1768 and Samuel Norman's bankrupt stock had been advertised for sale in London during December 1767, it can be surmised that this was the source for the bed.

To support this great final statement, there was a pair of magnificent *bombé* commodes (now in the Yellow Drawing Room) that were entirely decorative and part of the 'parade' furniture of the State Apartment *(fig. 115)*. As Cullen wrote in his letter to the Earl: 'these in grand apartments are more to furnish and adorn than for real use.' The Earl's decorator states, 'I have made some very fine ones of this kind for Ld Walgrave', but it seems most likely, as with his other acquisitions, that he procured them from a London maker of quality. They have the rhythm and swagger of a John Linnell design with prominent hips placed above a wide body. Two further features which point to this English maker are the long, single upper drawer over a panelled front and the rococo conceit of 'stretched holes' in the frieze. In this case, the holes can be seen as fresh air between the mounts and the carcase on its upper corners. It is a motif that is repeated in the matching pair of night tables also supplied by Cullen. Whoever was the maker of these very distinctive commodes, it is certain that they were specially commissioned for Hopetoun and not bought from stock. In common with many examples of fashionable furniture made for Scottish patrons at this time, the decoration incorporates a Saltire, the flag of Scotland, here prominently inlaid into the front panels.

Furnishing gathered momentum in the early nineteenth century with the preparation of the Red Drawing Room and new State Dining Room (in the place of the old State Bedroom) for a visit by Leopold, Prince of Saxe-Coburg-Saalfeld, in September 1819. This involved extensive re-gilding and the provision of new carved gilt cornices and picture and glass frames, as well as marble work by Edinburgh craftsmen David Hatton, David Ness, and John Steell. The celebrated Edinburgh firm of Young and Trotter, who had worked at the house providing bedroom furniture, upholstery, and Drawing Room items since 1767, supplied new informal Drawing Room furniture in oak, rosewood, gilded wood and marbled wood during the summer of 1819. This commission included two fine centre tables, one of which was an 'Octagonal Marble Slab supported by massive gilded trusses resting on a marble wood, plinth with gilded milled balls with a rich brass border'. These were in appropriately princely taste, anticipating the visit of King George IV to Hopetoun on 29 August 1822.

chapter 8

The Paintings Collection

by Christoph Martin Vogtherr

From about 1700, the collection of paintings at Hopetoun has evolved with the house itself. Different generations of the Hopetoun family have developed it in quite distinct ways, directly linked to phases of the construction and refurbishment of the building. The close relationship between the two is less visible today but becomes apparent when viewing the contributions of different generations as well as the considerable impact of sales and losses. Throughout the eighteenth and nineteenth centuries the collection at Hopetoun was clearly conceived as part of the interior decoration rather than as an independent entity. It was assembled to complement a house that was intended to demonstrate the importance of the family. The history of the collection exemplifies some of the most important developments in British eighteenth- and nineteenth-century collecting, and a more detailed examination will show the different phases of its history.[1]

Lady Margaret Hope, mother of the first Earl, signed the contract for William Bruce's first house in 1698. Between 1703 and 1705—therefore in the context of the achievement of Bruce's main building—Philip Tideman (1657–1705) painted a series of mythological and allegorical works for the first Earl of Hopetoun (1681–1742) which were sent to Scotland from Amsterdam.[2] Tideman's own list of thirty-seven paintings for Hopetoun—preserved in the archives of the house—specifies their subjects and sometimes the place for which they were intended in the staircase and in the apartments of Lord and Lady Hopetoun.[3] The iconography of the paintings was clearly linked to their intended location—e.g. paintings of Penelope, Alcmene, and Lucretia were to adorn the Lady's Chamber (Drawing Room) as *exempla* of female virtue while paintings of Scipio and of *Apollo Competing against Pan* and *Youth Forsaking Lust (fig. 116)* were commissioned for Lord Hopetoun's Drawing Room. The works were hung as overdoors or overmantles in the two apartments. Their architecturally defined location was a necessary component for a very specific iconographic programme. Eighteen of these paintings are still at Hopetoun whilst about half disappeared before the Second World War. The picture collection in the first house would mainly have consisted of these decorative paintings and family portraits. But little is known about any further, more substantial collecting activity.

Overleaf
Detail of *Four Brothers of the Manaldini Family* by Bartolomeo Passarotti

172

The first important collector in the history of the wider family was James Johnstone, second Marquess of Annandale (1688–1730). He bequeathed his important art collection to his sister Henrietta who had married the first Earl of Hopetoun. Annandale travelled abroad at least three times and is recorded as being in Italy from 1718 to 1720 and again 1729 to 1730, the latter stay being cut short by his premature death in Naples. Whilst abroad, he amassed large numbers of paintings, drawings, prints, books, and classical antiquities.[4] His nephew, the second Earl of Hopetoun (1704–1781), also spent time in Italy in 1715–1726. Their Italian acquisitions were shipped to Scotland as part of the same transports. When Annandale's collection passed from his own house Craigiehall to the second Earl, their joint collections implanted a distinct flavour of the Grand Tour at Hopetoun.[5] Both included sixteenth- and, more importantly, seventeenth-century Italian works, and acquisitions from living painters complemented these groups. The vogue for Italian art at the time covered the period from the High Renaissance (earlier examples were rare) to the contemporary. Major examples of the first group are Bartolomeo Passarotti's *Four Brothers of the Manaldini Family (fig. 117)*, first mentioned in the Great Dining Room at Craigiehall (acquired as a work by Agostino Carracci) before the painting came to Hopetoun, and Emilio Taruffi's *Two Boys with a Parma Boar Dog (fig. 118)*, which was in the Drawing Room at Craigiehall before it was brought to Hopetoun. Other typical examples of the period's taste are works by the contemporaries Carlo Maratta (he had only recently died at the time of Annandale's and Hopetoun's visits to Italy), Giuseppe Chiari, Francesco Trevisani, Benedetto Luti, and Paolo de Matteis. Most of them are no longer represented in the Hopetoun Collection.

The new plans for the house by William Adam (from 1721) introduced a different type of interior, with larger rooms and plain wall surfaces designed for the more concentrated and more prominent display of art works. The increased splendour and size

▲ *fig. 117*
Four Brothers of the Manaldini Family. Painting by Bartolomeo Passarotti

➤ *fig. 118*
Two Boys with a Parma Boar Dog. Painting by Emilio Taruffi

of the rooms required a very different type of collection to that of the old house. The bequest of the second Marquess of Annandale's collection provided an impressive corpus while the acquisitions of the second Earl himself in Italy were certainly made with the new plans for future rooms in mind. Later, in the years between the first Earl's death and the establishment of the new rooms, he tried to complete an ambitious acquisitions programme and prepare the first comprehensive display of the transformed and dramatically expanded collection. Records of several auctions from the 1740s and 1750s at which the Earl was a buyer are preserved in the Hopetoun archives: the Dalrymple sale of 1742, the Balmerino sale of 1746, and the Urquhart sale of 1757.[6]

An inventory of the Hopetoun collection from 1753 includes two columns for the actual and the intended locations of the work, providing an invaluable record of the very detailed planning process for the new state rooms.[7] Another inventory had been drawn up one year before but did not yet indicate the future location. We can assume that these two dates roughly mark the moment when precise plans for the furnishing of the new rooms were drawn up. The main rooms for the picture collection in the new Adam apartment became the Hall (for family portraits), the future Yellow Drawing Room (the "Saloon"), and the adjacent Red Drawing Room. Tideman's works and other decorative paintings remained in the Bruce rooms.

In the middle of the eighteenth century, the profile of the collection was distinctly international and included many of the most celebrated painters of the mid-eighteenth century, particularly Italian and Flemish masters. In Italy in 1725–6, the second Earl and

▲ *fig. 119*
The Arch of Titus in Rome. Painting by Charles-Louis Clérisseau

▼ *fig. 120*
The Temple of Antoninus and Faustina in Rome. Painting by Charles-Louis Clérisseau

fig. 121
The Death of Lucretia.
Painting by Gavin
Hamilton

fig. 122
Dutch Shipping in a Stiff
Breeze. Painting by
Ludolf Backhuysen

the Marquess of Annandale apparently shared similar tastes. The former had possibly returned to Italy in 1737–8 but, by the time his collection was catalogued in 1752 and 1753, a noticeable change had occurred. An important number of Netherlandish paintings, in particular a whole group of works by David Teniers, had been added. The more prominent taste for Flemish painting was in line with recent developments in French and German collecting.

His two sons, Charles (1740–1766) and James (1741–1816, the future third Earl), went to Italy in 1762–4, by which time the new rooms in Hopetoun had been finished. A set of landscapes with Roman monuments by Charles-Louis Clérisseau reflect their decidedly neo-classical, typical Grand Tour taste *(figs. 119 and 120)*.[8] The two brothers were painted with their tutor William Rouet in Italy by Nathaniel Dance, a painting that came to Hopetoun in the twentieth century *(fig. 132)*. In 1763, Charles commissioned a major work from Gavin Hamilton, *The Death of Lucretia (fig. 121)*, which was finished in 1767 but was sold in the early nineteenth century on Andrew Wilson's advice.[9] While their Grand Tour obviously had an impact on Hopetoun, the third Earl does not seem to have pursued collecting, although a detailed inventory of the collection was drawn up in 1808.[10]

The death of the third Earl in 1816 was a turning point in the history of the Hopetoun picture collection. Almost immediately, the fourth Earl (1765–1823) began to reassess the collection and to shape it according to his own taste. In 1817, he called in the landscape painter and art dealer Andrew Wilson (1780–1848) to inspect the picture collection and charged him with the restoration of the paintings. Wilson later became the artistic advisor to the fourth Earl.[11] In his assessment of the collection, he recommended disposing of many works that had been acquired earlier and now reflected the old-fashioned taste of the first half of the eighteenth century. Many important works, mainly by eighteenth-century Italian painters, were sold along with Gavin Hamilton's *Lucretia*. Wilson proposed works by Titian, Veronese, Rubens and van Dyck as new cornerstones of the collection as well as masterworks of Dutch Golden Age painting. The seascape with *Dutch Shipping in a Stiff Breeze* by Ludolf Backhuysen *(fig. 122)*, today in the Yellow Drawing Room, bears witness to this scheme of acquisitions. Wilson's objective was obviously to bring the Hopetoun collection in line with the dominant aristocratic taste of the early nineteenth century, formed by the 'Orléans generation' (named after a consortium of British aristocrats who bought the collection of the Duke of Orléans in 1792). This taste included a penchant for Italian High Renaissance paintings and mainly seventeenth-century works of the Italian as well as Dutch and Flemish Baroque. The most prominent Netherlandish works at Hopetoun testify to this chapter of acquisitions, a part of the collection which was begun prior to the mid-eighteenth century but raised to a new level by the fourth Earl. The collection now made the major transition from a collection primarily of classically inspired contemporary art to an Old Masters collection. This campaign coincided with major changes leading towards the establishment of today's Dining Room in the North Wing and a major rehang of the fundamentally redefined collection. When visiting Hopetoun today it is evident that Wilson's activity also involved extensive reframing, as the large number of late Georgian frames in the house

fig. 123
The Adoration of the
Shepherds. Painting
by the workshop of
Peter Paul Rubens

fig. 124
Detail from the
frame of the
Adoration

testify. The *Adoration of the Shepherds* by the workshop of Peter Paul Rubens *(fig. 123)* provides a splendid example *(fig. 124)*.

Several sets of drawings document the different hanging schemes. The most comprehensive set shows the new arrangement of the collection made after Wilson's changes. For the first time, these drawings included the new Dining Room, hung as today with a group of important family portraits—second only to the grouping in the Hall. But the set of drawings also covers the Saloon, Red Drawing Room, the Hall, and several smaller rooms in the old house. One earlier hang is also documented comprehensively, possibly dating from the time before the present Dining Room was established. This set of drawings (double lines marking the size of the paintings) covers the Saloon *(fig. 125)* and Red Drawing Room. Both picture arrangements are comparable in style, symmetrically covering the wall surface as densely as possible. It is likely that these two undated sets of drawings were created within a short span of time.

One much earlier arrangement is also documented in a drawing. In the Red Drawing Room *(fig. 126)*, the wall above the chimney piece is empty, and was possibly being occupied later by Hamilton's *Lucretia*—an indication that it might date from before 1767 (when the painting was finished) and was part of the plans for the first hang. This earlier arrangement is not only different because of the paintings included, but also because of its very distinct aesthetic impact. The overall impression is much more spacious, leaving more of the wall surface visible with the paintings arranged in a much more architectural way. Its style is that of the eighteenth century, very different from the arrangements documented by the other two sets of drawings which follow aesthetic ideals of the nineteenth century. This earlier version, possibly the first hang, is directly informed by the design of the new rooms and must have been conceived when they were still new.

The early nineteenth century marks the beginning of the collection's dispersal. At the instigation of Andrew Wilson, the fourth Earl sold a large part of the eighteenth-century collection.[12] The whole character of the collection changed and now had a contemporary flavour. Sales of lesser paintings[13] in the twentieth century seemed to have been caused primarily by financial necessities, particularly around the time of the Second World War, and were discretely arranged. Later, isolated exceptional paintings were sold, most importantly van Dyck's portrait of the Marchese di Spinola *(fig. 127)* and Canaletto's *Molo from the Bacino di San Marco*.[14]

fig. 125
Hanging arrangement of the pictures in the Saloon, nineteenth century

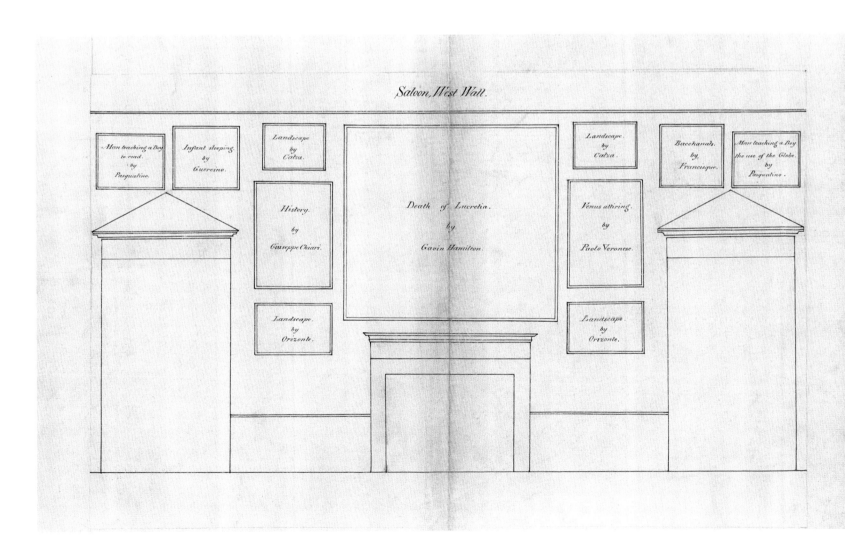

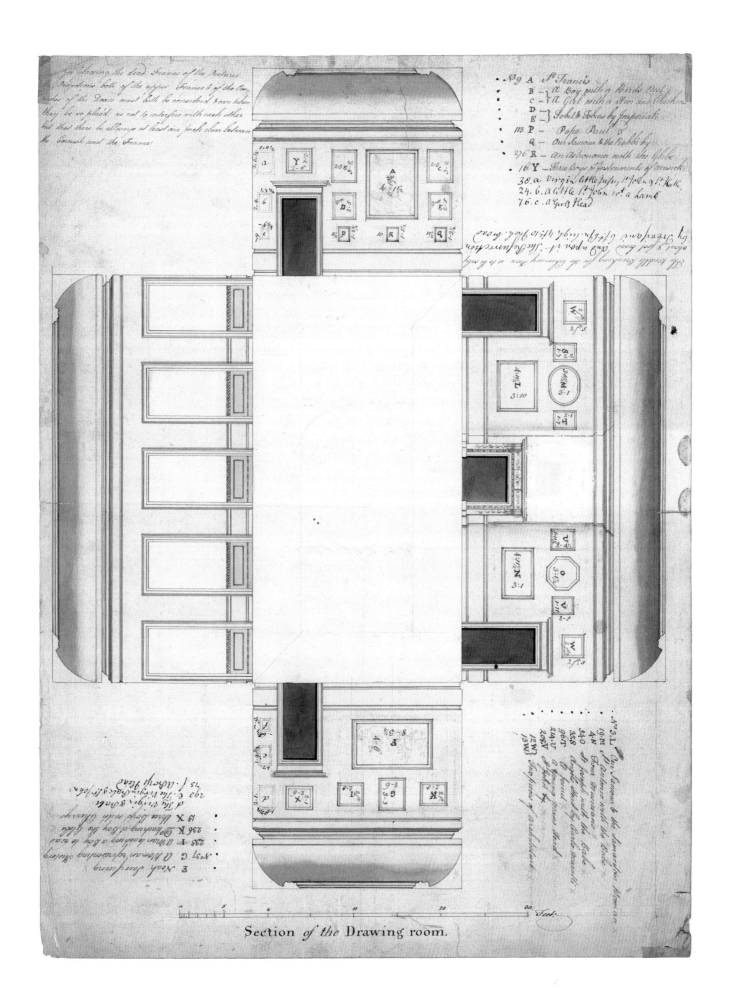

Section *of the* Drawing room.

fig. 127
The Marchese
Filippo di Spinola.
Painting by
Anthony van Dyck

The collection in Hopetoun has evolved significantly over the years, as is typical for most British country houses. But generational differences are particularly obvious. The present collection at Hopetoun is a multi-layered entity which incorporates examples from different periods of collecting—still an impressive ensemble, but not one that is necessarily easy to read.

◄   *fig. 126*
Hanging arrange-
ment in the Red
Drawing Room,
eighteenth century

chapter 9

The Family Portraits

by James Holloway

'At Hopetoun House in the county of Linlithgow, the princely seat of the Earl of Hopetoun, is a numerous collection of portraits', wrote Sir William Musgrave in the last decade of the eighteenth century. Over 200 years later, Hopetoun retains its numerous family portraits in a collection that both adorns the house and illustrates many of the most important men and women interwoven with Hopetoun's long history.

Sir William Musgrave, that inveterate enthusiast for portraiture, would recognise many of the paintings he listed, particularly that of Sir Thomas Hope of Craighall, 1st Bt (1573–1646), Lord Advocate of Scotland, attributed to the founder of Scottish portrait painting, George Jamesone; as well as the portraits of his sons, Sir John and Sir James. Sir John's portrait was painted by Jacobus Schuneman, Sir James's by Jamesone. Sir James *(fig. 2)* was the first member of the family to style himself Hope of Hopetoun. In 1678 he married the heiress Anne Foulis and with her came great wealth, in particular the acquisition of the rich lead mines of Lanarkshire. In due course Sir James's son John acquired land at Abercorn near South Queensferry on the Firth of Forth, but John died prematurely, drowned while accompanying the future King James to Scotland in 1682 *(fig. 4)*. He left a widow, Lady Margaret, and an infant son, Charles. No doubt it was John's intention to build the family seat on the newly acquired Abercorn property, but the project was started by Lady Margaret and the contract with her architect Sir William Bruce was signed in 1698. It was actively progressed by Charles as he grew to manhood. With wealth, an impressive new house and a position as Member of Parliament for his county, Charles was created first Earl of Hopetoun in 1703. Other honours, including the Order of the Thistle, followed. Charles's Countess was the daughter of the first Marquess of Annandale, Henrietta Johnstone. The Earl and Countess are the subjects of a pair of portraits by William Aikman, Scotland's leading portrait painter from 1710 until he moved to London about ten years later *(figs. 5 and 6)*. His portraits of the Hopetouns are excellent but perhaps not on an adequately grand scale to satisfy later members of the family.

Much more imposing is the great full-length portrait of the first Earl, painted after the Earl's death by David Allan, who by the late 1770s had become a favourite of the

Hopes *(fig. 128)*. Allan used Aikman's contemporary portrait as the base for his likeness. The Earl is portrayed at leisure at Hopetoun (but in his peer's robes and wearing the chain of the Thistle), inspecting plans of his new building while masons are at work outside on the construction of the north wing. He has volumes of Palladio and Vitruvius close at hand and Allan has taken care to dress Lord Hopetoun in the costume of his time.

Family friendships, political alliances, and marriage brought other portraits into the newly built house. A fine example is Sir John de Medina's portrait of the first Earl of Seafield, who was both a political connection of the first Earl of Hopetoun and the father-in-law of his daughter Sophia. Charles's marriage to Henrietta forged a very close link between the Hope and Johnstone families. Henrietta's brother, the second Marquess of Annandale, travelled to Italy between 1717 and 1720 and amassed one of the largest collections of artworks ever assembled by a British Grand Tourist. The unmarried Marquess left it to his nephew John, the eldest son of Charles and Henrietta, having become mentor to the young man. Included in the gift was his magnificent full-length portrait by the Roman painter Andrea Proccacini (1718), in which he is shown admiring a few of the objects that he had collected in Italy *(fig. 129)*. Following the advice of his uncle, John also travelled widely there, visiting numerous cities. He had his portrait painted by Marco Benefial in 1726 and acquired many works of art. Not only was he interested in art, he also visited

fig. 128
Charles, first Earl of Hopetoun. Painting by David Allan

fig. 129
The second Marquess
of Annandale. Painting
by Andrea Procaccini

186

hospitals and other institutions. When the time came for the city of Edinburgh to build a new infirmary, James, second Earl, as he was later styled, became the hospital's principal benefactor, giving an annual donation of £400 towards the care of incurable patients. The building and equipping of Edinburgh's Royal Infirmary became a national project and Lord Hopetoun's generosity would certainly have encouraged others—the artist Allan Ramsay for example, whose grandfather and great-grandfather had been employed as factors on the Hopetoun estates. He chose to paint the second Earl in his grandest manner and in 1748 made a gift of the portrait to the hospital as his personal contribution to the popular national project. Ramsay of course knew that his portrait would be seen by every visitor to the new hospital and could not fail to be helpful in furthering his career.

Ramsay's portrait remains the property of the Royal Infirmary, but many years later his only equal as a portrait painter in Scotland, Sir Henry Raeburn, was asked to copy it. Raeburn's copy has never left Hopetoun and hangs in the State Dining Room *(fig. 130)*. A few years earlier, Ramsay had painted another portrait of the second Earl, a handsome painting that remains at Hopetoun. It probably marks James's accession to the earldom in 1742 and was originally paired with Ramsay's portrait of the new Countess of Hopetoun, James's first wife, Lady Anne Ogilvy. Lady Anne's portrait is no longer at Hopetoun, and Ramsay's portrait of the Earl now hangs alongside Thomas Gainsborough's delightful portrait of the Earl's second wife, Jane Oliphant

fig. 130
The second Earl of Hopetoun. Painting by Henry Raeburn after Allan Ramsay

(fig. 131). The Gainsborough probably dates from 1762, the year she became Countess of Hopetoun. There are also pastel portraits of James and Jane by William Hoare, who worked with Gainsborough in Bath in the 1760s. It is likely that the second Earl and his Countess were painted there. David Allan's portrait of Charles Hope-Weir, the brother of the second Earl and the man who had travelled to Italy with Robert Adam on their Grand Tour, also hangs in the Dining Room *(fig. 7)*.

If Procaccini's portrait of the Marquess of Annandale records the early years of the British Grand tour, three great portraits by Nathaniel Dance were done at the high-water mark of Great Britain's engagement with her classical past. Outstanding in size and ambition are two full-length portraits of the brothers, Charles, Lord Hope, and Captain James Hope. Painted in 1763, they intentionally rival the work of Rome's leading portrait painter, Pompeo Batoni. Dance was still in his twenties when they were painted and comparatively unknown, but the brothers' choice of artist was both brave and successful. Charles looks pale and tired in his portrait, and indeed he died three years later. In contrast, James, an officer with the 3rd Regiment of Foot, appears hale and confident. It was he who succeeded his father to the earldom in 1781. The two young

▲ *fig. 131*
Jane, Countess of
Hopetoun. Painting by
Thomas Gainsborough

▶ *fig. 132*
The brothers Charles and
James Hope with their
tutor William Rouet on
their Grand Tour. Painting
by Nathaniel Dance

men and their tutor William Rouet are the subject of the third of Dance's portraits—this is much smaller but it shows the men amongst the buildings and artefacts that they were in Rome to study *(fig. 132)*. William Rouet was a learned man and had been Professor of Oriental Languages at the University of Glasgow until he resigned to accompany the Hopes to Italy. In Dance's group portrait the three men are overshadowed by a colossal antique vase; in the background appears the dome of St Peter's. The setting combines aspects of modern and ancient Rome to make the point, as no doubt their tutor would have informed the brothers, of the continuity of civilisation and their part in it.

Nathaniel Dance spent twelve years in Rome, returning to Britain in 1766. The following year a young Scottish artist, David Allan, set sail for Italy where he remained for ten years. Allan was born at Alloa on the Firth of Forth, a few miles upriver from Hopetoun. Supported by local families, the Cathcarts and Erskines in particular, he flourished in Rome and Naples winning prizes and gaining a name for himself in particular as a painter of small domestic and conversational paintings, to use his own description. It was in Rome in 1773 that he met and painted Henry Hope and his tutor John Gillies, a portrait that now hangs at Hopetoun. But it was not until he returned to Scotland in 1777 that his very close association with the Hope family developed fully. During his first winter back home, Allan, unused to the cold, fell ill, whereupon his aristocratic patrons rallied round. One such was Lady Charlotte Erskine, a sister of the second Earl (and therefore aunt of Charles, James, and Henry). The Hope family quickly became Allan's main patrons, even welcoming him to Hopetoun to spend his winters there. The house still contains many of his paintings, the most impressive being the posthumous portrait of the first Earl, already referred to. The most engaging of all is probably the double-portrait of Ladies Jemima and Lucy Hope, daughters of the third Earl, which today hangs in the Library. Allan found further patrons for his portraits through the family and their friends and relations and the Hopes actively canvassed for him when Allan put his name forward to become the salaried Master of Scotland's only school of industrial design, The Trustees' Academy in Edinburgh.

Sir Henry Raeburn has been mentioned as the artist who copied Allan Ramsay's full-length portrait of the second Earl which hangs in the Dining Room. He also painted the fine portrait of another member of the family, Charles Hope, Lord Granton, President of the Court of Session. It was in the Yellow Drawing Room, on 29 August 1822, that Henry Raeburn was knighted by King George IV, using Sir Alexander's own sword. John, fourth Earl, his Countess, and his brother Sir Alexander had welcomed the King to Hopetoun at the end of a hugely successful state visit; the Sovereign's arrival at Hopetoun is recorded in a watercolour by Dighton showing the steps of the house lined with members of the King's bodyguard in Scotland, The Royal Company of Archers, with

▲ *fig. 133*
John, fourth Earl
of Hopetoun, in
archer's uniform.
Painting by Watson
Gordon

➤ *fig. 134*
The first Marquess
of Linlithgow.
Painting by Robert
Brough (detail)

the Scots Greys and the West Lothian Cavalry in attendance *(fig. 11)*. Sir Alexander is the subject of two dashing portraits: the earlier by the Austrian artist, Friedrich Heinrich Fuger (1801), the other by Raeburn's great English contemporary, Sir Thomas Lawrence (1810). The Earl and his brother, both generals, had been very distinguished soldiers; indeed, the Duke of Wellington said of the Earl that he was the ablest man in the Peninsular Army. He commanded the Royal Company of Archers, and it was in his Archer's uniform, as Captain-General, that he sat to Sir John Watson Gordon *(fig. 133)*. After Raeburn's death in 1823, Sir John became Scotland's leading portrait painter and the first President of the Royal Scottish Academy. He also painted the glamorous portrait of another hero of the Peninsular War, Lord Macdonald of Sleat, whose portrait in the

fig. 135
The second Marquess
of Linlithgow. Painting
by Oswald Birley

collection can be explained by the fact that Macdonald's daughter, Louisa, married the fifth Earl of Hopetoun—yet another man who sat to Watson Gordon.

The fifth Earl's grandson, the seventh Earl and another John, was created first Marquess of Linlithgow in 1902. An eminent courtier and politician he became Governor of Victoria in 1889, remaining in Melbourne for six years and returning to Australia in 1900 as the first Governor-General and Commander-in-Chief of the new Australian

fig. 136
Lord and Lady Hopetoun
with their children.
Painting by Richard Foster

Commonwealth. His importance in the family story is reflected in a magnificent full-length portrait by Robert Brough *(fig. 134)*, an excellent Edwardian portrait painter whose promising career was cut short by his death in a railway accident. Brough's portrait was painted in 1904, a few months before he died. Two versions were made, one for Hopetoun, where it remains, the other for the Town Hall in Linlithgow. At six foot five inches the second Marquess cut an imposing figure and, as Britain's longest-serving Viceroy of India, he had if anything an even more distinguished diplomatic career than his father. His period in office, from 1936 to 1943, covered the very difficult years leading up to Indian independence. His portrait by Sir Oswald Birley of 1945 *(fig. 135)* hangs opposite the portrait of his father in the Entrance Hall while the prime version is in Rashtrapati Bhavan, formerly the Viceroy's house, in New Delhi. Portraits of more recent members of the Hope family are on display at Hopetoun. The present Earl, Andrew Hopetoun, his Countess Skye, and their young family have recently been painted by Richard Foster *(fig. 136)*. Their eldest son and heir, Charles, Viscount Aithrie, is the subject of Sergei Pavlenko's dashing full-length portrait *(fig. 137)*. These vibrant paintings, amongst others, bring the collection of family portraits at Hopetoun thoroughly up to date.

fig. 137
Charles, Viscount
Aithrie. Painting
by Sergei Pavlenko

chapter 10

The Revival of the Walled Garden

by the Countess of Hopetoun

Whwhen my father-in-law decided to move out of Hopetoun in 2006, one of our initial concerns was where we could have a garden. At Philpstoun, our home for eight years, we had begun to make a traditional British garden with roses, lavender, peonies, irises, vegetables, and a cutting garden. We loved it: there was always something for a vase, it was small enough to maintain with only very occasional part time help, and most importantly the children had somewhere they could run around to their hearts' content. The house at Hopetoun stands alone surrounded by gravel and lawn, a testament to the eighteenth-century landscape design unaltered by nineteenth-century borders or terraces. I have grown to love the appropriateness of our new home's surroundings from an historical point of view, but this, the 100-odd events held at Hopetoun a year, and the six-month open season make family life with children and dogs rather harder—especially for someone used to privacy.

I spent hours doodling away, plotting gardens close to the house wherever I could find a hidden spot. Despite the large scale of the grounds, there just didn't seem to be anywhere suitable to create a new family garden. For some extraordinary reason, I never considered the old walled garden until my husband suggested it.

The walled garden at Hopetoun runs to some twelve acres, making it, I gather, the largest in Scotland. The wall is well over a kilometre long, broken by five gates and three doorways. Although loved and gardened by the family until the 1970s, in 1978 the garden was leased as a garden centre. A successful business was established and the garden was maintained. Then, in 1998, the Garden Centre, now called the New Hopetoun Gardens, moved to another site on the estate which suited better and freed up the garden for more appropriate use within an historical context. Dreams were hatched of a nineteenth-century recreation. Unfortunately the huge funding needed to facilitate that scale of project never emerged, so the garden was left abandoned and deserted, with the only maintenance being the mowing of the lawns. The abandonment lasted a full eight years. In 2006, when I first looked into it with a view to taking the garden on as a project, and as a bolt hole for my children, it was a struggle to walk around. Weeds, self-seeded shrubs (especially the ubiquitous buddleja), broken glass, and abandoned greenhouses dominated *(fig. 138)*.

Overleaf
A detail in the Walled Garden

196

Naively, but with enthusiasm fuelled by a combination of ignorance and large scale vision, I began to clear the garden. At the beginning it was just me, clearing away, cutting back buddleja and chainsawing shrubs. One night, one of the greenhouses I had been clearing fell down completely; thank goodness no one had been inside. Whilst this was going on I was trying to write a PhD thesis and bring up four small children, at that stage between the ages of four and eight. Something had to give: eventually, reluctantly, the research into Scottish Rococo plasterwork was put into long-term abeyance and the garden began to dominate my thoughts.

We had totally underestimated the scale of the job. Even just bringing the garden back to a workable form involved more manpower and money than I had ever imagined. What was at first estimated to be three large skips of hardcore, brought in by the garden centre and excavated by us, turned out to be thirty. For years I was given diggers plus a driver for a set number of weeks for my birthday or Christmas. Little envelopes would be opened with 'HAPPY CHRISTMAS—you can have Rab and a large digger for two whole weeks' *(fig. 139)*.

Again the estimated length of time was never even close to what was actually needed, but bit by bit we started getting there. The main gate was another birthday present, and the kitchen in the Bothy was given for Christmas. Outbuildings were restored with the help of a grant and a very generous husband. Greenhouses were re-glassed, restored, or removed. One greenhouse was donated to an enthusiastic gardener in Fife to help him start a nursery business.

In actuality it was probably no bad thing that the clearing took so long. During that time

fig. 138
The state of the garden before the intervention

my perception of what I was trying to create totally changed. At first I had envisaged a Secret Garden–style romantic garden, very much in the traditional British style but with less formality. I wanted the garden to look like an aged beauty, with the structure and definition still visible, but shrouded by softer planting. The plants were to be textbook Vita Sackville-West or Lawrence Johnson. It was to look like a once-great garden showing its former glory in a dishevelled and colourful way. I had no idea how much maintenance and money that would involve. Despite a diploma from the Inchbald School of Design I was planning the impossible, and the more I read, the more I wanted to look for something new and achievable.

Books began swarming into the house in huge numbers; the 'people who bought this also bought' section on Amazon has a lot to answer for. I began with the basics: William Robinson was the obvious place to start considering my aims, but Beth Chatto and Christopher Lloyd also became firm favourites. The first plantings were influenced by them and others and were rather obvious. A car park was dug up, new soil imported, and roses, nepeta, box, and lavender planted. Another area was created very much in the style of the Prince of Wales's yew walk at Highgrove. A rectangle of pleached limes was planted where the old display beds had been, in which drainage tubes were used as randomly placed ponds surrounded by concentric circles of box radiating out like the ripples on a pond in rainy weather. They were pretty, but not exactly exciting or innovative *(figs. 140 and 141)*.

Most of my plants were bought cheaply from various nurseries for budgetary reasons; the downside of this is that you are never quite sure what will arrive. The white *paeonia*, which I had ordered 100 of, turned out to be various shades of pink—not the end of the world, but not what I had planned. While I was still in my lavender-admiring stage, 200 white *lavendula* turned out to be blue. Again this didn't matter in the grand scheme of things, but I was beginning to want to do my own style of planting, things less obvious, less commonly used in Britain, and to my newly-informed eye more appropriate. I was being seduced by the New Perennial Movement and was avidly reading the works of Henk Gerritsen, Piet Oudolf, and Noel Kingsbury. I became adamant that I wanted to create a new style of garden: more environmentally friendly, more sustainable, more naturalistic, and in my view more attractive throughout the year.

The garden is still very much in embryonic form. It will take many decades before the vision I have is realised, but there are areas that are beginning to take shape. The new perennial planting on the terrace is particularly pleasing to me. Influenced by the planting style of Piet Oudolf and also by an old black-and-white photograph of the herbaceous border at Kinross in the 1920s, I wanted to create a low maintenance, old-fashioned herbaceous border—but using new plants, in a muted palette, all of similar heights and all flowering at the same time late in the season. I sent a list of my plant suggestions to Chris Marchant of Orchard Dene nursery, who couldn't believe I hadn't

fig. 142
The central Beech
Circle looking towards
the Cherry Orchard

seen her catalogue—she had most of the plants I was after and has since become my most favoured supplier and a huge ally and friend. Chris also helped simplify the shapes of the planting blocks. You cannot see that the underlying plan is geometrical, but it did make it easier to lay out and plant. Early interest comes from a mass planting of tulips, followed by alliums, but come August it really begins to take shape and life. The interest continues throughout the winter as nothing is cut back, and all the plants have been selected to stand without staking. The border is over 60 metres by 16 metres and needs very few hours to keep it in shape; in February it is cut back and mulched, but apart from that very little weeding or maintenance is needed *(Plate XXI–XXIII)*.

The beech border is a similar idea, traditional in structure but with modern, low maintenance plantings in reds and pinks *(fig. 142)*. I am pleased with it, even though it

fig. 143
The Cottage Knot

hasn't run its length; hopefully it will be finished soon. The dominant plants are *persicaria, thalictrum, eupatorium, sanguisorba,* and *miscanthus,* so the height is quite a feature, with only a narrow path down the middle. It will eventually lead to the already planted cherry avenue, which at the time of writing stands in a field of weeds but will shortly be transformed into an unusual meadow of *paeonia* and *camassia* and a perennial seed mix from Pictorial Meadows, a company founded by that genius of Sheffield, Professor Nigel Dunnet—now known by most people as a creator of the Olympic Park planting schemes.

Other areas of the garden are progressing with varying degrees of success. The cottage knot *(fig. 143)* is doing what it is supposed to—providing colour throughout the season in an easy blend of low maintenance cottage perennials. The Luciano border is less of a triumph, which serves me right as I had basically plagiarised another design. I will have to rethink it this season: the *deschampsia cepitosa* that self-seeds to the point of being a nuisance will be used elsewhere, and the replacement *briza medea* will hopefully do the job better.

One of the most unusual plantings replaced the old rose border. It consists of sections of plants randomly mixed within defined areas. The colour is mainly soft white, but there are a very few gentle exceptions *(Plate XXIV)*. Some people may consider it a mess, but this garden is fundamentally being created for me to enjoy with my family. If other people appreciate what I am trying to achieve, then that is an added bonus, but not the object of the exercise. Luckily one of my influences, Noel Kingsbury, seemed to understand fully my aims and objectives. He published my very amateur plan on his blog, quoting 'A lady and a garden to watch', and as an American commentator points out, 'being noticed by Noel Kingsbury is having your work noticed as (planting) art history'. This planting will blend into two adjacent areas, one planted with magnolias (tiny at the moment, but they will grow) with wild white under-planting, the other a more fantasy area created by mounding the soil into rounded abstract forms. White-stemmed birches have been planted, some of which will be multi-stemmed, and the planting is mainly of woodland grasses and ferns, with a creamy white colour palette as a defining aspect.

I am also experimenting with scattered seed mixes of my own making, using native local perennials, as opposed to the bought mixes used in the cherry orchard. So I have spent hours searching through native wildflower books singling out the ones from this area that I like. I have put these into three complementary groups which I plan to scatter in a camouflage pattern adjacent to the arboretum. This was an area of commercially planted spruce and larch, which has now been cleared and is slowly being replanted with specimen trees. Although there is an obvious and rather harsh line between this and the arboretum, I was interested to see late-nineteenth-century photographs showing that it was always thus. From the terrace, the view of the new wildflower area (not a meadow, as I am not using any grasses) will, I hope, be magical. To the east of this, still within the garden wall, my parents are creating an incredible plantsman's garden, with extraordinary attention to detail and horticultural knowledge. It is simply beautiful already, and, embarrassingly, was started at the same time as I began my project, but now appears to be years ahead.

The beautiful arboretum to the south of the walled garden is slowly being cleared, and eventually paths will be created with woodland, and shade-loving plants will be encouraged. There will be a camellia walk and also a fern area. Hopefully it will look natural and beautiful as well as being a wildlife haven.

Pam Lewis woke me up to the importance of insects in the garden and the environment, and it is something I feel very strongly about. When I began gardening in the walled garden I rarely dug up a worm, and, believe it or not, the birdsong was minimal. Now the borders positively hum with insect life, more than I have ever come across elsewhere, especially in my newer plantings. The combination of that with the fact I think all the new planting is pretty makes me feel I am on the right track. Of course it goes without saying that none of this would be possible without the very generous support of my husband and the constant enthusiasm of our gardener, Caryn Farquhar, who maintains a positive attitude despite weeks of neglect. Although I am not able to spend as much time in the garden as I would like, it is my constant companion. Once the projects in the walled garden are finished, I plan to move onto the western valley between the grounds and the park. I already call it the Himalayas, perhaps slightly prematurely. Then there is the marvellous bandstand and the utterly collapsed Norwegian hut, the very grand Italianate staircase and the bog-wood walk to tackle.

Living at Hopetoun is a joy, and gardening is my passion. These projects will presumably keep me occupied well into my dotage.

▼ *fig. 144*
Plan of the Walled Garden by Jemima Coulson

➤ *fig. 145*
The Persicaria River with stepping stones

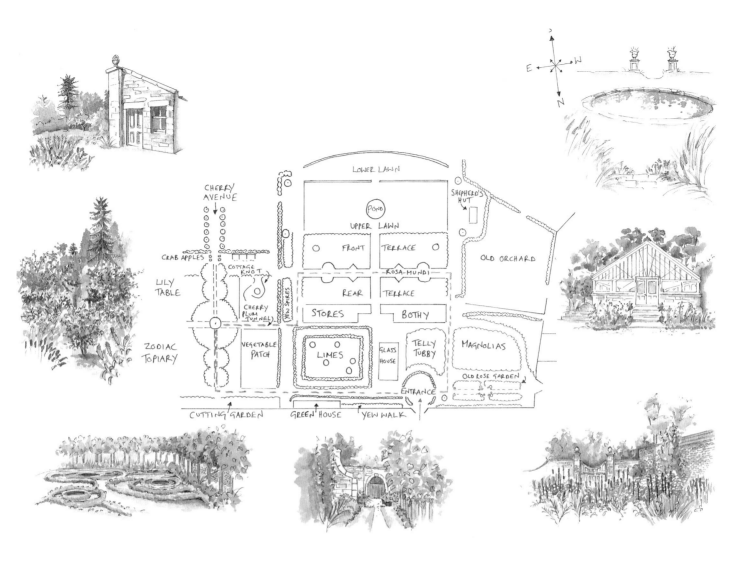

CHERRY AVENUE

LOWER LAWN

SHEPHERD'S HUT

POND

UPPER LAWN

CRAB APPLES

FRONT TERRACE

OLD ORCHARD

LILY TABLE

COTTAGE KNOT

ROSA MUNDI

YEW SPIRES

CHERRY PLUM TUNNEL

REAR TERRACE

ZODIAC TOPIARY

VEGETABLE PATCH

STORES

BOTHY

LIMES

GLASS HOUSE

TELLY TUBBY

MAGNOLIAS

OLD ROSE GARDEN

ENTRANCE

CUTTING GARDEN

GREEN HOUSE

YEW WALK

N S E W

chapter 11

Hopetoun
Present and Future

by the Earl of Hopetoun

I find myself writing a vision for Hopetoun's future whilst reading about the aftermath of the terrible fire at Notre-Dame de Paris. We had our own fire here, in March 1973, when the southern end of the main house was gutted, the blaze tearing through the family apartments such that afterwards one could stand at ground level within the building and see the sky. We were profoundly lucky that there was very little wind that day; the fire was halted before it spread north into the main part of the house, and the two pavilions were untouched; but we lost many things of great importance to us, of sentimental (and in some cases no little financial) value, if not of equal cultural significance to the contents of the State Apartments.

An occurrence like that makes one think deeply about the importance of a building, and there was never any doubt in my father's and grandfather's minds but that the damaged section should be rebuilt. This took the next four years, and those formerly damaged parts continue to provide a home for the Hopes, testament to the correctness of the decision. The redecoration that followed the rebuilding was carried out by Colefax and Fowler, not long after the retirement of John Fowler *(Plate XXVII and fig. 146)*. The result is that our private apartments are a mix of (relatively few) pre-fire interiors with the majority of rooms having been decorated between the 1970s and the modern day. These contrast with the rest of the house and its mix of original Georgian interiors and Regency and later updates. When we moved into the house in 2006, with my father moving into the very lovely house on the estate where our children had grown up, our bedroom had been decorated thirty years previously. We redid it recently, and I hope very much that it will last in its current form another 40 years, although it is perhaps too much to expect of it the 250 years or more achieved by much of the Red Drawing Room silk.

Hopetoun, built by Sir William Bruce and the Adam family between 1700 and *circa* 1755, is a place of great natural and man-made beauty, a country house showing off the best of British classical, Baroque, and neo-Classical architecture. It is at heart a home, and is of great importance to many of my family members, all of whom have a strong feeling of belonging and a sense of place here.

Hopetoun, though, is more than a home. It is an historic building, amongst the most important in Scotland and the UK and a repository for much history and many

Overleaf
View of the three
Forth bridges, with the
allegory of Hope in the
foreground

fig. 146
Family drawing room,
rebuilt and decorated by
Colefax and Fowler after
the fire of 1973

fig. 147
The cafeteria in
the former stables

beautiful things. For seventy years or so, it has been a visitor attraction and a place of business, and it is also a community, giving employment, involvement, volunteering opportunities, and more to a wide group of people *(fig. 147)*.

The House and its immediate grounds are owned by a Scottish charity, the Hopetoun House Preservation Trust. This entity was created in 1974, the year of the Victoria and Albert Museum's landmark exhibition *The Destruction of the Country House*. This highlighted the phenomenon of the twentieth-century demolition of country houses across the United Kingdom for social, political, and financial reasons, and caused a significant re-evaluation of the roles of these places in the fabric of our country. As *Our Place in Time*, Scotland's 2014 strategy for the historic environment, puts it, 'The historic environment is part of our everyday lives. People cherish places, and the values of the historic environment lie in defining and enhancing that connection of people to a place.'

My grandfather said in 1982 about the creation of the Preservation Trust: 'Great changes were necessary if Hopetoun was to survive and continue to hold its place in the Scottish cultural scene; and great changes have indeed taken place.' The intention of the Trust was to

> preserve the house and grounds as a national monument and to protect and improve their amenities; to preserve for the benefit of the nation the furniture, paintings, manuscripts and other articles of historical or artistic interest associated with the house; and to facilitate and encourage access to the house and grounds, and the study and appreciation of the House and its contents and of the ancillary buildings of historical interest as well as the designed landscape surrounding the house for educational purposes and in particular, for purposes connected with historic or aesthetic education.

To date, Hopetoun has survived and held the place it has had for the last 300 years; I remain positive and optimistic about the next 300.

The estate that surrounds the house, and other estates in Scotland, remain in the ownership of the family and provide context, as well as the financial resources to support work on the house in the way that they did in the past. The reliance on minerals (primarily shale, coal, and lead workings) has long ceased, but a mixed rural estate, combining agriculture, forestry, property, tourism, and other businesses, remains a strong and resilient diversified family business. This generates a solid core of revenue and allows us to re-invest and support other established businesses, start-ups, community and charitable endeavours, and the like, and to sustain the designed landscapes and other historic properties that form such an important element of Hopetoun's character *(figs. 148 and 149)*.

We are fortunate in Scotland to have a very large number of historic properties. Traditionally built dwellings form one in five of our built housing stock, many from Glasgow's tenements and Edinburgh's New and Old Towns but also in rural areas across the country. There are 47,000 listed buildings and 8,000 scheduled monuments. I am determined that Hopetoun retains its place amongst the foremost of them. As a lived-in family home, Hopetoun offers something unexpected to many people, and it is interesting to contrast the way in which previous generations lived in these houses and how they are used and inhabited now. There are striking differences: many fewer domestic staff, the sharing of spaces with visitors or wedding parties, the six months of the year we spend as a day-visitor attraction, and the consequent lack of immediate outdoor privacy, for example. But there are also similarities and, to me, one of the extraordinary things about these buildings is their very great flexibility in being able to offer a home both to seventeenth-century and to twenty-first-century families.

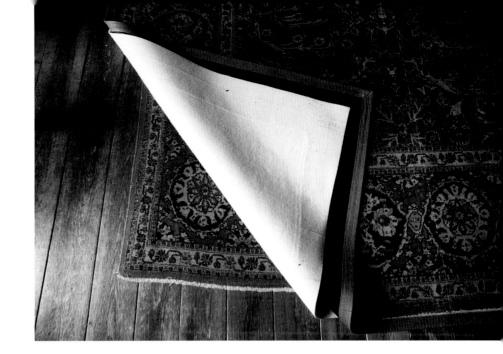

Hopetoun also houses an important collection. From the earliest acquisitions and commissions through to the Cullen furniture made for the house and still in the rooms for which it was made, as well as more recent portraits and the newly acquired carpet replacing the very worn one in the State Dining Room *(see also fig. 150)*, this collection shows the choices and preferences of one family over 300 years of its history. It is very important that the collection continues to evolve, sometimes to replace items lost (for example in the 1973 fire) but more often because we have acquired or commissioned something to which we are drawn.

Hopetoun is deliberately shown to our visitors as it is, a family home. We hope they feel as though they have come to see us and get a flavour of how the family did, and still do, live in the house. We have resisted wider diversification. Jimmy Douglas-Menzies, for many years both factor of Hopetoun Estates and secretary to the Hopetoun House Preservation Trust, put it like this:

> The deliberate policy at Hopetoun, adopted by the family and followed by the Trustees, has been to eschew any temptation to establish a Wildlife Park or the like at Hopetoun, or other forms of commercial entertainment, in order to attract more visitors. It is considered that that sort of thing would be quite out of keeping with Hopetoun and would eventually defeat the whole object of preserving the place for cultural education and aesthetic enjoyment. I am certain that future generations as well as the present one will applaud this policy and be grateful for it. As general development in Central Scotland continues to increase there will be more and more people yearning for peace and beauty and some dignity in a world which will become increasingly rushed, clamorous and ignoble.

It is very hard for me today to disagree with anything he wrote almost 40 years ago.

The word 'balance' is one that seems to recur endlessly to Hopetoun's General Manager and me when we describe Hopetoun and how it operates. Any vision must include the balancing of different, and occasionally competing, interests—access and conservation, exclusive event business and the day visitor, home and place of work, light damage and appreciation of contents, and so forth. We hope and believe that we strike a sensible balance on all of these, and thus allow the house to contribute responsibly to its own conservation and maintenance.

Another word that is often used is 'authenticity'. People are quick to notice the staged, the inappropriate, or the jarring—so a vision, whether formally expressed and publicised or simply shared by those involved, needs to be coherent and comprehensible. I hope that the clear message of a family home, with a collection and a setting as envisioned by its first owners and its architects, presented by those proud of its history and its contemporary place, is one that can be felt here.

◄ *fig. 148*
One of the cottages at Midhope

▲ *fig. 149*
Estate buildings modernised and let for offices

▲ *fig. 150*
An Eyemat floor covering, printed with an image of the original, a protective covering for the historic carpet in the Red Drawing Room

fig. 151
The three Forth
bridges seen from
the Estate

I am very fortunate in that the character of Hopetoun and our experiences over the last fifty years clearly inform the vision for the future. Its location twelve miles or so from Edinburgh city centre and just to the west of the (now three) Forth Bridges *(fig. 151)* creates opportunities for commercial activity that would be much harder were we to be in a more remote location; and the ballroom, in the south pavilion and able to seat 300 for dinner, provides a fantastic setting for such activity. The house's business balances commercial events and a limited number of weddings with six months of being open to visitors, tours, and visits out of season by appointment, as well as some extremely popular public events such as our fireworks display and the Christmas Fair. These provide, as I write, a steady and growing income which allows the generation of a surplus to be spent on improvements to the condition of buildings and contents.

We were fortunate that we were able to replace entirely the lead on the main house not long after a post-war low. At that time, the leadwork on much of the roofs had failed (not least thanks to the damage inflicted by hot shrapnel fragments falling from the defence of Rosyth against enemy aircraft) and was replaced by felt, which was all that could be afforded at the time. The roofs of the pavilions were addressed in the 1980s and 1990s, and the main house roof was reworked in the early 2000s, as was much of the house's stonework *(figs. 152 and 153)*. These more major projects were sometimes supported by public and other bodies with funds that are now spread increasingly thin as demand increases and broadens with time. The result of these and of the ongoing lower-level works is that the outer skin of the buildings is in good condition. We work hard to keep it that way.

▲ *fig. 152*
The lead roofs and
the stonework of the
façades—a never-ending
maintenance task

➤ *fig. 153*
Plaque documenting
the repair of the
lead roof in 1985

fig. 154
A remote part of
the grounds

Use of space is of great importance. Having lived through one fire, none of us wishes to see a repeat. Other risks are sadly very familiar to so many of us in our homes: wear, fungal or insect ingress, weather damage, and the like. A primary defence against such threats is for rooms and areas to remain in use, with their temperature and humidity managed, and regular visual inspection. The quick overview of ceiling, windows, radiators, and walls when entering a room becomes an unconscious habit. In all cases, though, we try to find an appropriate use and one that fits the wider Hopetoun character. The aim, on finishing a project, is for even the first-time visitor to feel that it must always have been like that.

Elements of our strategy seem clear to us. There is a happy confluence of cost saving and environmental good practice in the deliberate decision to leave parts of the grounds (out of view of the house, whose setting is paramount) relatively less kempt *(fig. 154)*. Walk round them first thing in the morning, and birdsong amply demonstrates the value of the habitat. Other advantages are more unexpected; recently we have been the fortunate beneficiary of the large number of visitors, many from overseas, who come to sites used in the filming of a television series set in the time of the Jacobite conflicts *(fig. 155)*. Generally, though, the strategy for the house is to continue to build

fig. 155
Midhope Castle—
recently used as a
TV and movie
location

its reserves whilst investing in vital (and even sometimes optional) maintenance; recently, the focus has been on the unglamorous but very necessary rewiring of the main part of the house for the first time since the 1950s. As part of this process, we are, for example, replacing lights with more energy-efficient and longer-lasting equivalents, but we are also trying to maintain the fitments, switches, etc., as they are part of the character of the place. All these decisions will be very familiar to the custodians of other such houses, and I would not say that there is anything wildly innovative in what we are doing. We are trying to maintain the highest standards, with the best available advice, as has hopefully always been the case.

Hopetoun's great strength, other than the beauty of its setting, has always been its people. To our teams across house and estate, and to the large number of volunteers, some of whom have been involved here since the earliest days of the Hopetoun House Preservation Trust, we remain deeply indebted. We are very grateful to all those who visit Hopetoun, hold events here, and contribute to the upkeep of this amazing house.

Each generation creates something and adds a layer to Hopetoun. We hope our layer is positive.

XXVII   The family
         drawing room

XXVIII The china room

XXIX Enfilade from Lady Hopetoun's dressing room

XXX   The gun
room

References

Chapter 2

1   Mappe of Wast Lothian comonly called Linlithgowshire / authore Johanne Adair. National Library of Scotland Adv.MS.70.2.11 (Adair 8) and A Map of West Lothian / survey'd by Mr. J. Adair. [Edinburgh : Cooper, c. 1737] National Library of Scotland EMS.s.737(17)

Chapter 3

1   The word 'aisle' is used in two senses in this chapter. Generally it means a space which follows the axis of the building from west to east, on one or both sides of the central 'nave', and in the middle ages was used for processions or extra accommodation. There is usually a chapel at the east end of the north or south aisles. In post-Reformation Scotland, where liturgical processions would have been unthinkable, the term 'aisle' was used to describe a place of burial for a land-owning family and all three principal variations are found at Abercorn church: one kind has the burial place below and a prominent family pew above, looking into the church; another kind is physically attached to the wall of a church but is walled and roofless; another kind is walled and roofless but not attached to the church.

2   References for this chapter:

Hope Papers Trust at Hopetoun House, historic archive of the Hopes of Hopetoun

The Gardens of Hopetoun—A Story of Development and Change, Hopetoun Research Group Studies, Trustees of Hopetoun House Preservation Trust

The Lettering Arts Trust website for information about the collaboration of poet, Ian Hamilton Finlay, with sculptor, Nicholas Sloan

Colin McWilliam, *Buildings of Scotland, Lothian except Edinburgh*, Penguin Books, 1978, and especially for Christopher Wilson's essay on 'The Medieval Churches'

Howard Colvin, *A Biographical Dictionary of British Architects 1600–1840*, 4th ed., Yale University Press, New Haven & London, 2008

Chapter 5

1   For more on the architecture of Hopetoun, see James Macaulay, *The Classical Country House in Scotland 1660–1800* (London, 1987); James Macaulay, 'Sir William Bruce's Hopetoun House', in *Architectural Heritage* 20 (2009), 1–14; Alistair Rowan 'The Building of Hopetoun House', in *Architectural History* 27 (1984), 183–209; Deborah Howard, 'Sir William Bruce's Design for Hopetoun House and its Forerunners', in Ian Gow and Alistair Rowan (eds.): *Scottish Country Houses 1600–1914* (Edinburgh, 1998).

2   Macaulay, *Classical Country House*, 81 fn.3.

3   Ibid., 56. Macaulay lists the defects of Floors Castle.

4   There are close parallels to Lord Leicester at Holkham and his architect Matthew Brettingham, a trained bricklayer. Much like Adam, Brettingham never had a single original idea about architecture but made a successful career on the basis of what he had learned at Holkham. Adam had the advantage of profiting from a second learned patron after Hopetoun, Sir John Clerk of Penicuik, for whom he executed Mavisbank. See also James Lees-Milne, *Earls of Creation: Five Great Patrons of Eighteenth-Century Art* (London, 1962).

5   Colin McWilliam, *The Buildings of Scotland: Lothian except Edinburgh* (1978), 253.

6   Superimposing the new layout on the earlier one published in *Vitruvius Britannicus* shows that significant sections of the outer walls are in the same position, suggesting that at least the flanking pavilions of the Bruce layout were executed and their fabric reused. Rowan suggests that the two bays of the west façade directly adjoining the main block at its southeast corner remain from Bruce's corner pavilion.

7   John Macky, *A Journey through Scotland* (1723), 200ff. It is described 150 years later in another travelogue as a 'princely mansion'; see John William Small, *The Castles and Mansions of the Lothians* (1883), 1.

8   William Adam, *Vitruvius Scoticus: Plans, Elevations, and Sections of Public Buildings, Noblemen's and Gentlemen's Houses in Scotland* (Edinburgh, 1812).

9   Rowan 'The Building of Hopetoun House', 195.

10   Rowan 'The Building of Hopetoun House', 196.

11   In his design for Newliston, William Adam proposed an ideal version of the arrangement of Hall, Tribune, and Saloon; see Adam, *Vitruvius Scoticus*, pl. 33.

12   Katherine Eustace, 'Robert Adam, Charles-Louis Clérisseau, Michael Rysbrack and the Hopetoun Chimneypiece', *Burlington Magazine*, Vol. 139, no 1136, 1997, 743ff.

13   Ibid., 748.

14   Sebastian Pryke, 'Furniture Designs from Hopetoun House', *Furniture History*, vol. XXVIII (1992), 35ff.

15   Adam Nicolson, *Men of Honour: Trafalgar and the Making of the English Hero* (London, 2005), 166.

16   Hopetoun Archives, NAS GD18/4783, 9 August 1755.

Chapter 6

1   Helen Hughes, 'The Problems Facing the Development in Architectural Paint Research' in Helen Hughes (ed.), *Layers of Understanding: Setting Standards for Architectural Paint Research* (Dorset: Donhead Publishing Ltd., 2002), 13.

2   Franz Mairinger, 'Technologische Untersuchungen an Wandmalereien', in *Restauratorenblätter*, 9 (1987), 16.

3   K. Clark, 'Architectural Paint Research in a Wider Context' in Hughes (ed.), *Layers of Understanding*, 4.

4   'Period before a given date' and 'period after a given date', respectively.

5   Sebastian Pryke, 'A History of the Interior Decoration and Plenishings', Hopetoun House Archive (unpublished report, 1998), 20. According to Pryke, the yellow damask was likely manufactured in the third quarter of the nineteenth century. Ian Gow believes the design represents a palm; see Ian Gow, 'An Opinion of Hopetoun House', Hopetoun House Archive (annex 9, unpublished report, 1998), 19.

6   Hopetoun House Archive, box 60/12.

7   Hopetoun House Archive, bundle 621.

8   Pryke, *History of Interior Decoration*, 7. Pryke's notes on John Paterson are based on Hopetoun MSS bundle 147/373.

9 Hopetoun House Archive, bundle 640; account is dated 24 June 1768. According to Pryke, most of the State Apartment was painted by McLaurin; see Pryke, *History of Interior Decoration*, 7, based on Hopetoun MSS bundle 147/640.

10 Samples No. 3 and 36 (see appendix 1).

11 On the terms 'white-washing' and 'whitening', see I. C. Bristow, *Architectural Colour in British Interiors 1615-1840* (New Haven and London: Yale University Press, 1996), 47.

12 *Hopetoun House* (Derby: Heritage House Group Ltd., 2004), 11.

13 Bristow, *Architectural Colour*, 60, 71.

14 According to Pryke, this room is the 'Saloon'; however, the 'Saloon' was gilded and painted in 1827, and the ceiling had been painted with an oil colour. This document is dated April 1828; see Hopetoun House Archive, box 87, bundle 1.

15 From the 1740s on, this type of wallpaper was also used in representative rooms with the flocked surface imitating brocade; according to J. Cornforth, *Early Georgian Interiors* (New Haven and London: Yale University Press, 2004), 194.

16 Bristow, *Architectural Colour*, 150.

17 Black bole was in fact a greyish bole used in England in the nineteenth century; see J. Simon, *The Art of the Picture Frame* (London: National Portrait Gallery, 1996), 36.

18 Bristow, *Architectural Colour*, 98.

19 Cornforth, *Early Georgian Interiors*, 123; Bristow, *Architectural Colour*, 150.

20 Hopetoun House Archive, box 87, bundle 1; the works were executed in 1819, but the notes on expenses are dated April 1828.

21 Hopetoun House Archive, bundle 2950.

22 Hopetoun House Archive, bundle 2950 and bundle 3025; Bristow, *Architectural Colour*, 61.

Chapter 8

1 The family portraits in Hopetoun are of a very high quality but more or less typical for a major house in Britain. Acquisitions of sculptures and drawings were an equally essential part of the original fabric of the collection but will not be discussed here.

2 Basil Skinner, 'Philip Tideman and the Allegorical Decorations at Hopetoun House', *The Burlington Magazine* 106 (1964), 368-73

3 The Archive of the Hopetoun Papers Trust, bundle 635. The list specifies the intended location of the paintings as overdoors and overmantles.

4 John Ingamells, *A Dictionary of British and Irish Travellers in Italy 1701-1800*, New Haven/London 1997, 560. A list of his acquisitions in 1718-20: The Archive of the Hopetoun Papers Trust, bundle 1647; for 1728-30 (not 1729, as in Ingamells): ibid. bundle 1523; a short list of acquisitions: ibid., bundle 1657.

5 Inventories of works of art in Craigiehall: The Archive of the Hopetoun Papers Trust, bundle 1525 (inventory from 1725, before the last trip to Italy); bundle 616 (inventory of works of art in the Closet at Craigiehall, apparently not yet placed because of the Marquess's death); bundle 401 (list of works of art as appendix to the Marquess's testament).

6 The Archive of the Hopetoun Papers Trust, bundle 801.

7 The Archive of the Hopetoun Papers Trust, bundle 1525. The same bundle includes an inventory from 1752 which does not yet include information on the future location of the paintings.

8 They are mentioned in the inventory of 1808 as hanging in the Dining Room: The Archive of the Hopetoun Papers Trust, bundle 606.

9 John Ingamells, *A Dictionary of British and Irish Travellers in Italy 1701-1800*, New Haven/London 1997, 519-20 (Charles and James Hope). The painting is now in the Yale Center for British Art.

10 The Archive of the Hopetoun Papers Trust, bundle 606, cp. bundle 1606, an inventory which must have been made before 1818.

11 On Wilson and Hopetoun: Basil Skinner, 'Andrew Wilson and the Hopetoun Collection', *Country Life* (1968), 370-2.

12 The sale, London, 15 February 1832, also seems to have included Hopetoun paintings (e. g. Guercino's *Christ and the Woman from Samaria*). One copy of the sale catalogue is annotated with a reference to the Annandale collection (see Getty Provenance Index), although by that time the title had been extinct for several decades.

13 The Archive of the Hopetoun Papers Trust, bundles 805, 806, 1362.

14 The van Dyck (today in the Queensland Art Gallery, South Brisbane): Susan J. Barnes, Nore de Poorter, Oliver Millar, Horst Vey, van Dyck, *A Complete Catalogue of the Paintings*, New Haven/London 2004, 214-5, no. II.78; Canaletto: Joseph Gluckstein Links, *A Supplement to W. G. Constable's Canaletto: Giovanni Antonio Canal 1697-1768*, London 1998, 11, no. 106*.

231

Contributors

Anne Bantelmann-Betz is an art historian focussing on architectural history and conservation. Her doctoral dissertation on the reconstruction of classical English country houses destroyed by fire was published in 2013. She is professor of architectural conservation at the Hochschule RheinMain in Wiesbaden.

Peter Burman FSA has studied History of Art at King's College, Cambridge, and conservation of Mural Paintings at ICCROM in Rome. He has practised as an architectural historian and conservator. He has taught at University of York and BTU Cottbus and in between has been Director of the Church of England's central office for conservation of churches and cathedrals and Director of Conservation of the National Trust for Scotland. Currently he is on the Board of John Ruskin's Guild of St George and a member of the Fabric Committee of St George's Chapel, Windsor Castle. He is trustee of two great houses, House of Falkland and Hopetoun House. At Hopetoun he is also Honorary Archivist.

Christopher Dingwall is a freelance heritage consultant and lecturer with a special interest in the history of gardens and designed landscapes in Scotland. He served for twelve years as Conservation Officer with the Garden History Society in Scotland and is currently Vice Chairman of Scotland's Garden and Landscape Heritage.

Asita Farnusch trained as an architect and building archaeologist. A scholarship from the Fritz Thyssen Foundation enabled her to conduct extensive research into the construction history of Hopetoun, resulting in precise plans and sections of the existing building.

Polly Feversham holds degrees in History of Art and Architectural Conservation. With her husband, she helped to restore and run Duncombe Park in North Yorkshire. She co-edited the book on Holkham in 2005.

John Hardy FSA set up the archive in the Furniture Department of the Victoria and Albert Museum in the early 1960s, and later had responsibility for Osterley Park House. He contributed to the publication on Holkham Hall in 2005, and had previously helped with the arrangement of furniture at Hopetoun House. From 1990 he was a researcher in the Furniture Department of Christie's King Street.

James Holloway was the Director of the Scottish National Portrait Gallery for fourteen years and closely involved with Hopetoun House as a Trustee.

David Jones taught Furniture History at the University of St Andrews where he developed the study of Scottish furniture. He is Hon. Keeper of Furniture at Dumfries House, Ayrshire, and a member of the Conservation Panels at Hopetoun House and Paxton, Berwickshire. For Paxton, he has written a catalogue of the Chippendale furniture in their collection: *Neat and Substantially Good: Thomas Chippendale's Scottish Achievement* (2018). He is currently writing on the furniture collection at Blair Castle, Perthshire, for publication in 2020.

Leo Schmidt FSA teaches architectural conservation at the Brandenburg University of Technology in Cottbus. British country houses have long been one of his main areas of research, resulting in a book on Holkham (published 2005), edited jointly with Polly Feversham.

Alexandra Skedzuhn-Safir trained as an art conservator in Florence for works in stone and ceramics, later focussing on the conservation of architectural surfaces. As a lecturer in architectural conservation at the Brandenburg University of Technology, her interest lies in transdisciplinary approaches to heritage protection.

Christoph Martin Vogtherr is an art historian with a special focus on French eighteenth-century painting. He became Director of the Wallace Collection in London in 2011 before moving on to be Director of the Hamburger Kunsthalle between 2016 and 2019. He is now Director-General of the Foundation for Prussian Castles and Gardens in Potsdam.

Selected Bibliography

William Adam, *Vitruvius Scoticus: Plans, Elevations, and Sections of Public Buildings, Noblemen's and Gentlemen's Houses in Scotland* (Edinburgh, 1812).

Charlotte Bassett, 'A Revised Timeline for Sir William Bruce's Hopetoun House, 1699–1707,' *The Georgian Group Journal*, XXVI (2018), 1–20.

Katherine Eustace, 'Robert Adam, Charles-Louis Clérisseau, Michael Rysbrack, and the Hopetoun Chimneypiece', *Burlington Magazine*, 139, no. 1136 (1997), 743ff.

Deborah Howard, 'Sir William Bruce's Design for Hopetoun House and Its Forerunners', in Ian Gow and Alistair Rowan (eds.), *Scottish Country Houses 1600-1914* (Edinburgh, 1998).

James Macaulay, *The Classical Country House in Scotland 1660–1800* (London, 1987).

James Macaulay, 'Sir William Bruce's Hopetoun House', *Architectural Heritage*, 20 (2009), 1–14.

Colin McWilliam, *The Buildings of Scotland: Lothian except Edinburgh* (1978), 253.

Sebastian Pryke, 'Furniture Designs from Hopetoun House', *Furniture History*, XXVIII (1992), 35ff.

Sebastian Pryke, 'Hopetoun House, West Lothian', *Country Life* (10 August 1995), 44–9.

Alistair Rowan 'The Building of Hopetoun House', *Architectural History*, 27 (1984), 183–209.

Basil Skinner, 'Philip Tideman and the Allegorical Decorations at Hopetoun House', *The Burlington Magazine*, 106 (1964), 368–73.

Basil Skinner, 'Andrew Wilson and the Hopetoun Collection', *Country Life* (1968), 370–2,

A more detailed version of Lord Alexander Hope's chapter on the Hope family, including extensive references, will be made available on the Hopetoun website, www.hopetoun.co.uk

Index of Persons

Acknowledgements

The editors wish to express their gratitude to all those who made this book possible. Special thanks are due to the authors of the individual chapters and to the photographers for their strikingly beautiful images.

The trustees, employees, and volunteers of the Hopetoun House Preservation Trust, particularly Piers de Salis and his team, have provided invaluable assistance, as have the trustees and volunteers of the Hopetoun Papers Trust, including Peter Burman, Richard Gillanders, Linda Balfour, and Fergus MacTaggart in the archives.

From Australia, Kristal Buckley and Kent Wilson sent excellent photographs of the first Marquess's equestrian statue in Melbourne. We are grateful to Sophia Hörmannsdorfer, Lord Johnstone, Andreas Köstler, Tim Knox, Leonardo Leckie, Marita Müller, Jeremy Musson, and Antonia Reeve for their kind assistance and advice.

The Fritz Thyssen Foundation generously supported building archaeology conducted in the house.

The book has been long in the making—in fact it lay dormant for some years—but was saved by the enthusiasm and expertise of Thomas Zuhr of Hirmer and his colleagues Cordula Gielen, Lucia Ott, and Rainer Arnold. Thanks are also due to copyeditor James Copeland.

Colophon

Hopetoun: Scotland's Finest Stately Home

Published by
Hirmer Verlag GmbH
Bayerstraße 57–59
80335 Munich

Editors
Countess of Hopetoun, Polly Feversham,
Leo Schmidt

Authors
Anne Bantelmann-Betz, Peter Burman,
Christopher Dingwall, Asita Farnusch, John Hardy,
James Holloway, Lord Alexander Hope, Earl of
Hopetoun, David Jones, Alexandra Skedzuhn-
Safir, Christoph Martin Vogtherr

Project management
Cordula Gielen, Hirmer

Copyediting and proofreading
James Copeland, Berlin

Graphic design, typesetting, and production
Lucia Ott, Hirmer

Prepress and repro
Reproline mediateam GmbH, Munich

Paper
Gardamatt Art 150 g/m²

Printing and binding
Appl Druck GmbH, Wemding

Printed in Germany

Bibliographic information published by the
Deutsche Nationalbibliothek
The Deutsche Nationalbibliothek lists this
publication in the Deutsche Nationalbibliografie;
detailed bibliographic data is available online at
http://dnb.de

© 2020 Hirmer Verlag GmbH, Munich; and the
authors

ISBN 978-3-7774-3439-1

www.hirmerpublishers.com

Picture credits
The Annandale Collection: fig. 8
Frank Dalton: figs. 89, 90, 92, 96, 113, 145,
pp. 18–27, 50–55, 98–101, 138–145, 156–157,
224–229
Asita Farnusch/BTU: figs. 81, 95
Peter Keith: pp. 8–9
Monument Australia/Kent Watson: fig. 15
National Collection of Aerial Photography:
figs. 19, 21
National Army Museum London: fig. 10
National Galleries of Scotland: figs. 1, 60, 64,
National Library of Scotland: fig. 20
National Maritime Museum, Greenwich: fig. 4
Leo Schmidt: figs. 28–41, 51, 55–59, 62, 68, 70–73,
76–78, 84, 85, 93, 94, 104–106, 108–115, 147,
149–153, pp. 10–11, 12, 70–71, 86–87, 102–103,
212–213, 240
Alexandra Skedzuhn-Safir: figs. 98, 101–103
Queensland Art Gallery, South Brisbane: fig. 127
Claire Takacs: figs. 142–145, pp. 14, 195–196,
204–211
Wikipedia: fig. 45
Yale Center for British Art, Paul Mellon Fund:
figs. 3, 121
The Hopetoun Collection: all others

Cover: Aerial view of Hopetoun from the east,
Peter Keith
Back cover: Allegory of Hope, Leo Schmidt; In
the Walled Garden, Claire Takacs; The Red
Drawing Room, Frank Dalton; The Octagonal
Staircase, Frank Dalton
pp. 8–9: Aerial view of Hopetoun from the east,
Peter Keith
pp. 10–11: Hopetoun's east façade, Leo Schmidt
p. 12: Allegory of Hope flanking the east façade,
Leo Schmidt
p. 14: In the Walled Garden, Claire Takacs
pp. 232–233: View of Hopetoun from the west,
Peter Keith
p. 240: View along the southwest vista towards
Hopetoun, Leo Schmidt